ANNULMENT

ANNULMENT

Your Chance to Remarry
Within the Catholic Church

Joseph P. Zwack

*with C. Robert Nixon
and Roger D. Conry*

HarperSanFrancisco

A Division of HarperCollins*Publishers*

Designed by Donna Davis

Library of Congress Cataloging in Publication Data
Zwack, Joseph P.
   Annulment : your chance to remarry within the
Catholic church.
   Bibliography: p.
   1. Marriage—Annulment (Canon law) I. Nixon, C.
Robert.   II. Conry, Roger D.   III. Title.
LAW   262.9   83-47739
ISBN 0-06-250990-X

 95 96 RRD (H) 20

To Mom and Dad:
My successes are yours;
my failures are mine.

CONTENTS

Acknowledgments   ix

Introduction   xi

Chapter 1.   Straight Answers to the Questions Most Often Asked About Annulment   1

Chapter 2.   The Annulment Procedure: Step by Step   13

Chapter 3.   The Selection of Grounds and the Rise of the Psychological Cases   37

Chapter 4.   The Cost of an Annulment   71

Chapter 5.   The New Code of Canon Law   75

Chapter 6.   The Internal Forum and Other Approaches   79

Appendix I.   Canons on Marriage, New Code of Canon Law   88

Appendix II.   Sample Forms   104

Appendix III.   Volume of Formal Cases Presented for Annulment   122

Bibliography   127

ACKNOWLEDGMENTS

With his background in sociology, my good friend Roger Conry has been of invaluable assistance in his research and encouragement to follow through with this book. Without him I might well still be simply talking about the need for such a book. Bob Nixon became involved when Roger and I concluded that we needed the viewpoint of someone with a good working knowledge of non-Catholic religions. Because of Bob's postgraduate work in comparative religions and his book-reviewing experience, he fit the bill perfectly.

I would like to thank the Rev. Denis J. Araujo, Ph.D., a parish priest with extensive experience in counseling and sponsoring those seeking annulments, for his expert advice and enthusiastic support for a book of this kind. I also greatly appreciate the expertise and energy that my editor at Harper & Row, John Loudon, devoted to the book.

INTRODUCTION

There *had* to be a book on the subject.

I checked the local public library. Nothing. I checked the library of a local Catholic college. Nothing except very technical works, some of them written several decades ago. I checked the local bookstore. Nothing. I checked the bookstore indexes for recent books in print on the subject. Nothing by non-canon lawyers. By now my curiosity was aroused. I wrote to the Canon Law Society of America. I received back a nice letter from the Executive Coordinator of the Society, in which he states: "I am sorry that there are no books that I know of that would explain canonical juridical procedures in 'common everyday language.'" It seemed there were various technical works touching on certain aspects of Catholic dissolutions and annulments, including grounds and procedures, but such writings were for the most part, in the words of the Executive Coordinator, "for professionals."

The irony and the significance of the situation stunned me. Even though I am an attorney with 16 years of Catholic education, I did not qualify as a "professional" to whom any available works on the subject would have meaning, because they were all too technical. What about my clients, who have no legal training, but whose lives are directly affected by the divorce and remarriage question? I did eventually find a few scattered works on the subject, mostly written by canon lawyer priests. But they were not at all what I was looking for.

And so it was that this book was written.

I have a general law practice in the largely Catholic city of

Dubuque, Iowa, and for some time had been growing increasingly dissatisfied with my own attempts to answer clients' most basic general questions about the Catholic Church's annulment grounds and procedures. By the time a client in a civil divorce proceeding is granted a divorce, he or she has usually questioned the attorney from all angles. Whether a Catholic client is "in" or "out" with the Church after divorce or remarriage often affects many aspects of that individual's life, such as attendance by the children at a parochial or a public school, religious education of the children, inclusion of the Church in the individual's will or trust, planned place of burial, choice of hospital, charitable contributions to Catholic institutions, attendance at Mass, and participation in the sacraments. Questions about excommunication still haunt many Catholics after a divorce.

I had found that, at a time when there was about one divorce for every two marriages, I could not offer even the most general guidelines or preparation in many of these areas. The biggest mystery involved the grounds and procedures for annulment and dissolution. These "Catholic divorces" were being given upon grounds and procedures that had all evolved since I had graduated from a Catholic college in the early 1960s.

As I became more involved in the writing of this book I came to realize that even priests, if they are not involved in the specialized work on the Tribunals, are often confused about these matters, especially the grounds for the filing of petitions.

Perhaps this widespread ignorance of the Church's position in this area is the reason that, in spite of the incredible increase in the number of annulments granted in the past ten years, far fewer than 10 percent of divorced Catholic couples have sought to "get right" with the Church, even though about 80 percent of divorced Catholics enter into a second civil marriage. And despite quantum jumps in the annulment rates by the American Tribunals, the number of divorced Catholics remarrying outside the Church is increasing.

There are approximately 15 million divorced Catholics and children of divorced Catholics in the United States today (which is about equal to the total approximate population of the combined states of Alaska, Arizona, Delaware, Hawaii, Idaho, Maine, Montana, Nebraska, Nevada, New Mexico, North Dakota, Rhode Island, South Dakota, Utah, Vermont, Virginia, and Wyoming).

It is a fact that a large number of these people, feeling there is no place in the Church for them, simply join the ranks of the "fallen-away Catholics." The purpose of this book is to show exactly how a large percentage of these divorced Catholics can have their original marriages set aside by the Church. If they have remarried, this means they can become practicing Catholics again.

I am sure this book will be condemned by some as being a guide to loopholes in the existing Church law on annulments and dissolution. My feeling, however, is that I am simply publicizing the grounds and procedures for the more than nine out of ten divorced Catholics who have not taken advantage of their rights in the Church today. I am not saying that these procedures are the way the Church *should* deal with the issue of marriage, divorce, and remarriage. Criticism of existing procedures abounds. I have made little attempt in this book to discuss the philosophical questions surrounding the annulment process. I have tried, rather, to approach the situation as a lawyer attempting to give my client the full advantage of knowing how to exercise his or her rights under the law and procedures as they now stand.

Since I began this book, the Church has enacted a revised Code of Canon Law. This revised Code (the first since 1917) will become effective at about the same time as this book is published. So far as was possible, the changes in the marriage and annulment canons have been incorporated into this book.

I do not feel that the existence of a revised Code should be a reason for Tribunal officials to adopt a wait-and-see attitude about how to implement the New Code regarding the continued granting of annulments. I am, in fact, confident that this will not happen in most American Tribunals, which have traditionally been the most efficient and progressive in the world.

1

Straight Answers to the Questions Most Often Asked About Annulment

In answering questions about annulment, there is the temptation to hide behind canon law Code numbers and long footnotes. I am able to resist this temptation for two reasons: First, I am not a canon lawyer. Second, I am not talking to canon lawyers.

I. A FEW BASICS

Just What Is an Annulment?

An annulment is a declaration by a Tribunal to the Church that a marriage never legally existed as a sacramental union according to canon law.

What Is the Difference Between an Annulment and a Divorce?

A divorce is a dissolution by a civil court of an existing union; an annulment declares that there never was a valid union, despite appearances to the contrary. There are both civil law and Church annulments. We will, of course, be talking about the latter.

How Many Catholics Could File for an Annulment?

About 8 million living Roman Catholics have gone through

the process of civil divorce in this country. This number increases by approximately 250,000 annually. Almost every one of these people will need to obtain an annulment if he or she wishes to remarry within the Church and the divorced spouse is still alive.

Is It Only Catholic Marriages That Need to Be Annulled Before a Second Marriage Can Take Place?

No. The Roman Catholic Church considers *all* marriages binding and *all* marriages between baptized Christians to be at least potentially sacramental. So from the Church's point of view, all first marriages must be declared null by a Church court before a second marriage can take place. Obviously, two Muslims or two Protestants who wish to remarry are not going to worry about this, but if one of them is converted to Catholicism, any non-Catholic marriage must be set aside by the Church Tribunal before remarriage is possible. These converts add a small but significant number to the 8 million already mentioned who need to seek a Church annulment before remarriage within the Church.

If I Am Legally Divorced Why Do I Need an Annulment?

The Church does not consider the civil authorities capable of breaking the sacramental bond. In the eyes of the Church you are still considered married to your first spouse. If you are content to remain single the rest of your life there is no Church penalty for divorce, but if you ever wish to remarry you must have the first union annulled in the eyes of the Church. If you are divorced there is an eight-in-ten chance you or your former spouse will need to petition for an annulment someday, because those are the chances of your remarrying.

What If I Do Not Have My First Marriage Annulled?

You will not be able to marry in the Catholic Church. If you marry outside the Church, the Church will consider you to be living in an "adulterous union." That means you cannot receive the sacraments.

You Mean I Would Be Excommunicated?

No. You would still be allowed to attend Mass and participate to some extent in the life of the Church.

But Doesn't a Divorce Mean Automatic Excommunication?

This is a common misconception. There is no Church penalty for divorce. As long as you do not remarry, you may receive the sacraments and participate in the full life of the Church just as you would if you were not divorced. Many divorced Catholics quietly kick themselves out of the Church when there is no need. They are neither excommunicated nor barred from the sacraments. Much confusion stems from the fact that a divorced person who remarried *used* to incur the penalty of excommunication. This is no longer true.

Well Divorce Is Still a Sin, Isn't It?

No. This is another misconception. Divorce itself is considered neither right nor wrong. In fact, the Church fully recognizes that in many instances it is necessary to go through the civil divorce courts to protect one or the other partner in a failed marriage, and to provide for such things as child custody, child support, alimony, property division, and the like. The problem, as mentioned above, is when the divorced parties seek to *remarry* (as most do).

II. SIGNS OF CHANGE

You Said Before That Catholics Who Divorce and Remarry Are No Longer Excommunicated. When Did That Change Take Place?

In May 1977, the Catholic bishops of the United States removed the penalty of excommunication from Catholics who divorce and remarry.

How Could They Do That?

Excommunication for remarriage had been a rule only in

the United States, and only since 1884. The American bishops imposed this sanction and they had every right to remove it.

Does That Mean That Catholics Who Divorce and Remarry May Freely Receive the Sacraments?

No, and unfortunately this is where much of the present misunderstanding enters in. Even though Catholics who divorce and remarry are no longer automatically excommunicated, they still are not supposed to receive the sacraments unless their former marriages are annulled. This never-never land has led many anguished Catholics to say that for practical purposes they are almost as bad off as they ever were, despite the fact that they are not excommunicated.

What Is the Good of Not Being Excommunicated if a Person Still Cannot Receive the Sacraments? What Is the Difference?

Aside from the right to attend Mass, there is the clear invitation to divorced and remarried Catholics to fully return to the Church and seek to be reconciled with it. In other words, the Church wants you to seek an annulment if you are entitled to it. A door is being held open that for a long time was shut. In *Ministering to the Divorced Catholic*, Fr. Young quotes Bishop Cletus O'Donnel as saying

> Those who have remarried and may have incurred the Church penalty of excommunication should see in this decision to remove the penalty a genuine invitation from the Church community. It is up to them to take the next step by approaching parish priests and diocesan Tribunals to see whether their return to full Eucharistic communion is possible.*

So the Church Is Actually Encouraging the Seeking of Annulments?

While maintaining a firm position on the indissolubility

---

* Young, *Ministering to the Divorced Catholic, p. 259.*

of marriage, the Church has given every sign of being willing to grant annulments far more readily than in the past. The clearest indication of this has been the overwhelming increase in annulments over the past decade.

How Difficult Is It to Gain an Annulment?

One of the best-kept secrets in the Church today is just how easy it has become to have a marriage annulled. Statistics vary slightly depending on the source, but all sources show that there has been an absolute explosion in annulments. In 1968 only 338 annulments were granted in the United States. In 1978 there were some 27,670 granted,* an increase of 8000 percent. The latest available statistics from the Canon Law Society of America show that more than 58,000 formal petitions for annulment were filed in 1981. How many of these were successful is not known. Additionally, thousands of "informal procedure" annulments were granted, as will be discussed later.

Not only is the number of cases high, the percentage of successful petitions is up, too. In 1968, out of the few cases accepted for a ruling, only 25 percent were finally granted annulment. Now, in many jurisdictions, more than 95 percent of the petitions accepted for consideration are ruled upon favorably. So in the past decade alone, your chances of success in many Tribunals have increased from one in four to about nine in ten. The reasons for these increases will be explained later.

With This Many Annulments Being Granted, What Percentage of Divorced Catholics Is Seeking Annulment?

Statistics show that far fewer than one out of ten divorced Catholics have come to the Church Tribunal for a ruling.

Why Is That?

The main reason is lack of information. Most people simply don't know how much things have changed. Others, through misinformation, fear they have no case or believe they cannot afford it. This book has been written specifically to help the

* *Time, Feb. 25, 1980,* p. 40.

uninformed or misinformed Catholic who wishes to return to participation in the Church.

III. EXPLAINING THE CHANGE

Why Have Things Changed So Much Recently?

Mostly because of genuine pastoral concern. I mentioned earlier that there are about 8 million divorced Catholics in this country. A Gallup Poll in 1980 indicated that Roman Catholics are now just as likely to divorce as their non-Catholic neighbors. Since the Census Bureau indicates that about 40 percent of first marriages end in divorce, we know that 40 percent of all Catholic first marriages are likely to end in divorce. And, as stated earlier, statistics also show that about 80 percent of all divorced persons (including Catholics) remarry. Many of these divorced and remarried people and their families leave the Church simply because of the remarriage. The resultant decrease in parochial school enrollments, vocations, and financial and other support is being sorely felt by the Church. The Church is doing what it can to help these people return to the fold.

How Can the Church Dissolve So Many Marriages if Marriage Is Supposed to Be Indissoluble?

An annulment does not dissolve a marriage. It simply means that in the eyes of the Church there never was a sacramental marriage at all.

Are There Really Likely to Be Grounds for Church Annulment in the Average Divorce Case?

Yes, according to the experts. Msgr. Kelleher, who has for many years been an active advocate of improving the annulment process, says that some Tribunals seem to be operating on the premise that *every* broken marriage can be annulled. And Fr. Doherty quotes a Tribunal official speaking about broken marriages as saying, "There is no marriage which, giv-

en a little time for investigation, we cannot declare invalid."*
This may be a slight overstatement, but it points out that given
the prevailing attitude in many marriage Tribunals, almost
anyone who is divorced is likely to be judged as having sufficient grounds to petition successfully for an annulment.

Fr. Diacetis, President of the influential Canon Law Society
of America, feels that "more than three million divorced Catholics in the United States have a good case for annulment."** I
think that even this estimate is perhaps conservative.

Isn't This Just a Loophole Mentality? Doesn't It Amount to the Granting of Divorce Under Another Name?

There has been some concern over this question, and it has
even been expressed by the Pope; but the shift has come with a
changing emphasis in the Church's own understanding of what
a true sacramental marriage involves. The switch often has been
discussed as a change from a "contract" to a "covenant" model
of marriage. Whatever the theological implications, the practical
implication is that for canon law purposes it is harder to live up
to a covenant than to fulfill a contract. As a result, we are com-
ing to understand that there are fewer sacramental marriages
than we once believed. This distinction between contract and
covenant leads to some confusion because the Church and the
state have different definitions of marriage.

What Are These Different Definitions of Marriage?

The Church has a very distinct and elevated concept of marriage. Marriage is, after all, a sacrament instituted by God. The
state's position is that marriages are easily made and easily
broken. In recent years the Church has come to the position
that, while sacramental marriages are indeed unbreakable,
they are rarer than once thought. If, by civil standards, a marriage has irretrievably broken down, it is quite likely that by
current Church standards there was never a true sacramental
union. After an annulment, an ex-spouse is still considered to
have been once married by all secular standards. The Church

* Divorce and Remarriage: Resolving A Catholic Dilemma, Doherty, p. 101.
** Spain, National Catholic Reporter, March 4, 1983, p. 19.

is saying that the seeds of the breakdown were probably always there. It was only when those seeds bore the inexorable fruit of a broken marriage that the marriage's true invalidity became obvious. Something—undoubtedly one of the annulment grounds—stood in the way of the marriage becoming a lasting union. If it had not, there probably would have been no divorce. If the seeds of the marriage breakup were there from the start of the marriage, there probably never was the chance of having a true sacramental union, and thus there are provable grounds for an annulment.

But Won't This Notion Destroy the Catholic Belief in the Sanctity of Marriage?

Certain forces within the Church have visions of the family crumbling away because Catholics who have divorced and remarried are being encouraged to seek annulments. Some have a vision of dastardly husbands and wicked wives discarding loving, hard-working spouses and hungry children in order to fly from responsibility into the arms of secret lovers because of this broadened annulment policy. They see a tight, harsh annulment policy as the only inducement for spouses to toe the line. Four refutations of these fears are:

(1) Annulments are granted only after the parties have *already obtained* a civil divorce. In other words, there has already been a physical breakup of the family before the Church is asked to become involved in the annulment process in any way.
(2) Most divorces today take place because both partners have, at least in the end, found the union intolerable and detrimental to each other and the children. Not only is it rather rare for annulment petitions to be challenged by the former spouse, there is often enthusiastic cooperation.
(3) Those who wish to return to the Church through the annulment process are almost always genuinely committed people who take the Church seriously enough to wish for reconciliation. Often they have been living for years in stable second marriages.
(4) As statistics indicate, Catholics are divorcing and remarry-

ing at the same rate as the rest of the population. In fact, the point often has been made that a refusal to allow these people a real means of reconciliation only drives them and their families from the Church forever. The old threatened "stick" of an impossible annulment process is no longer a deterrent to Catholic remarriage.

IV. HOW THE CHANGE AFFECTS YOU

Who Decides if an Annulment May Be Granted?

The Diocesan Marriage Tribunal decides if an annulment may be granted. There is a Tribunal in every diocese.

What if I Think My Case Is Too Weak for Me to Receive an Annulment?

You do not have to decide that for yourself. There is no charge for calling a parish priest or even a member of the Tribunal. An Advocate will help you look over your case to see if, indeed, grounds for an annulment exist. Let the experts decide whether you have a case. If you have no case they will tell you. But if you are divorced, chances are good that you do have grounds for annulment. Chapter 3 of this book is intended to help you decide if you have grounds.

What if I Am Clearly at Fault in the Divorce?

The Tribunal is not interested in fixing blame. Tribunals today are, in fact, like most civil courts in this respect. Their purpose is to examine the validity of the marriage. The fact that one spouse is more at fault than the other no longer impedes his or her right to petition for an annulment. The court process itself will not attempt to prove guilt or hand out punishment. Actually, the fault of one party in a divorce may help form a major part of the proof of the invalidity of the marriage in the eyes of the Church. For example, assume that a marriage has broken up because of the husband's continuing sexual affair with an old girlfriend. His very acts of infidelity may well constitute much of the evidence that the marriage should be annulled because of "simulation of consent" by the husband as a result of his "intention against fidelity" (as will be explained in Chapter 3).

What if My Parish Priest Has Told Me I Have No Case?

Since the usual way to approach the Tribunal is through the parish priest, many potential petitioners have been discouraged by pastors who do not approve of or are uninformed about the way things have changed. I know of one woman who was discouraged by three separate priests and who later went on to receive an annulment quite easily. Please remember that the parish priest is not the final word on this. You do not have to accept his decision. As a member of the Church you have a legal right to present your petition for consideration. If you cannot find a sympathetic priest to help you, you can contact the Tribunal office directly.

But My First Marriage Lasted for Years, and We Had Several Children. How Can I Possibly Receive an Annulment?

This will make absolutely no difference. Many Catholics are under the impression that they must prove nonconsummation in order to be granted an annulment. This is false, and is a good example of the kind of misinformation I am trying to correct with this book. The fact that you have consummated your marriage (that is, had sexual intercourse) and even had children will not stand in the way of an annulment under most of the grounds now being used in American Tribunals.

Will an Annulment Make My Children Illegitimate?

No! This is another misconception. It was decided long ago that under canon law children of a putative marriage are legitimate. A putative marriage is one that is believed by at least one of the partners at the time to be a real marriage. Almost all annulled marriages fall in this category. The same rule of the legitimacy of children holds true, incidentally, in civil law annulment cases. And in any event a Church annulment does not even attempt to speak to the issues of legitimacy, laws of inheritance, and other civil domestic law issues.

Don't I Have to Get a Dispensation from the Pope to Receive an Annulment?

No. Certain rare types of cases can be decided only in Rome, but the overwhelming majority of annulments are granted by local Tribunals. The newly enacted Code of Canon Law requires a review of successful petitions, but this is done regionally, and it will be quite unusual for any successful petition not to be confirmed on review. (This is discussed later in greater detail.)

Will I Need to Hire a Canon Lawyer?

No. The Advocate for the Petitioner is assigned by the Tribunal. You neither hire nor pay your Advocate. In one of the documents Petitioners sign they are asked to indicate whether they accept the Advocate assigned by the Tribunal (see, for example, the Mandate on the form on page 108). If you reject the assigned Advocate, another will be selected.

Will I Have to Appear in Court?

Probably not. You will be interviewed early in the process by your Advocate or parish priest. Later, depending on the grounds selected, you may be interviewed again. But your presence will not be required at the actual hearing of the case except in extremely rare instances. There will be no face-to-face confrontation with your ex-spouse or humiliating questions from an opposing lawyer. The petitions, witness statements, and proceedings are kept confidential. Petitioners who have gone through both a civil divorce and an annulment say that the annulment proceeding is the more humane by far.

How Long Does the Process Take?

The average case takes between six and eighteen months. More complex cases may take as long as two years, but this length of time would be unusual today.

During the past dozen years the American Tribunals have been operating under streamlined procedures known as the American Procedural Norms (APN). Although the APN are now superseded by the New Code, the imprint of these streamlined procedures remains in the American Tribunals. Under the APN a petition for annulment was to have been accepted or rejected for action within 30 days, with a final decision to be made within the next six months. Even though the goal of six months was often not attained, most Tribunal officials did the best they could to meet it. The New Code's automatic review process should add no more than a month or two to the procedure.

Is the Process Expensive?

No. The myth of the expensive annulment has deterred many from looking into the process. Actually, compared to the civil process of divorce, it is quite inexpensive. (See Chapter 4 for further information about costs.)

How Likely Is It That My Petition Will Be Accepted for Processing?

According to Fr. Tierney in *Annulment: Do You Have a Case?* 90 percent or more of all petitions presented to the Tribunals are accepted and proceed to a decision.* I pointed out earlier that a very high percentage (more than 90 percent in many dioceses) of petitions that proceed to a decision are ruled upon favorably. Certain dioceses are notable exceptions, though, and these will be mentioned later.

What Do I Have to Do to Petition for an Annulment?

That is what this book is all about. Chapter 2 will give you a step-by-step guide to the annulment procedure and Chapter 3 will help you decide on the grounds for petitioning. In brief, two things are required of you to get things started.

(1) You must initiate the contact with the Tribunal.

(2) With the help of a parish priest or the Advocate assigned to you, a petition must be written up and submitted to the Tribunal.

* *Tierney, Annulment, p. 9.*

2

The Annulment Procedure:
Step by Step

I. THE TRIBUNAL

Once you have decided to seek an annulment, you must get in touch with the Tribunal.

A. What Is the Tribunal?

The Tribunal! The name conjures up images of the French Revolution, the English Star Chamber, or maybe the Spanish Inquisition. Really, there is nothing to fear. Simply put, the Diocesean Marriage Tribunal is a court of canon law. Its main function nowadays is the examination of broken marriages according to canon law. All dioceses have them and they are just rather dull offices of the diocese, staffed by various perfectly ordinary priests and laypeople.

At first glance, Tribunals may seem like civil courts. There are similarities: A petition is filed and official proceedings are carried out in much the same manner as in a civil court. Advocates prepare briefs and present evidence and arguments. Judges consider cases in light of precedent and the existing law. But there are differences, too. Confrontation with the former spouse is almost entirely absent. The sheriff's office does not serve papers; the spouse does not have to hire a lawyer; and many of the emotional strains of settling such issues as child custody and visitation rights, alimony, child support, division of family assets and liabilities, and court costs will all be behind you. The fixing of fault does not arise as a contested issue. Particular acts of one or the other spouse may well be examined, but only as they relate to establishing grounds for annulment, not for assessing blame. As mentioned before, personal appearances by you or your witnesses are very rare. Results are not a matter of public record or newspaper comment.

Make no mistake, though, about the fact that the Tribunals simply do not employ the same concept of due process that we're accustomed to in civil courts. But, all things considered, the annulment procedure is emotionally far less demanding than the usual divorce proceeding.

B. Who Makes Up the Tribunal?

The Tribunal, as mentioned earlier, is made up of both laypeople and religious. There are secretaries and receptionists as in any other office, and if you have any direct contact with the Tribunal it is often with them. But the officials who will eventually try and hear the case all have formal titles. The most important of these people are:

The Officialis Theoretically, the bishop is the Presiding Judge of the Tribunal. In practice, however, he gives the job to the Officialis. So from your point of view, the Officialis is the Presiding Judge of the Tribunal, with the powers of the bishop in the Tribunal. You undoubtedly won't see anything of him, but you may hear the name.

The Judges These are the priests who hear the cases and make the decisions. They are experts in canon law. In the past, their number would usually not have exceeded 12 in any diocese, and your diocese may well have fewer than this. Almost always they have other duties besides serving as Judges of the Tribunal.

Before the APN came into effect, three Judges were required for a decision. The APN speeded things up by allowing one Judge to enter decisions. With the demise of the APN, some people feared the process might slow down, because the New Code again requires a three-Judge panel decision; however, laypeople are now being encouraged to serve in greater numbers on the Tribunals. More lay involvement could greatly ease the workload under which many of the priests are laboring. Thus what might have been lost on the one hand is being compensated for on the other. But whether these laypeople will have to be canon lawyers—a requirement that would make the right of lay involvement as Judges practically meaningless—is yet to be worked out. At present, very few laypeople are canon lawyers.

The Defender of the Bond   The Defender of the Bond is the equivalent of the Church's prosecuting attorney. The Defender's job is to uphold the laws of marriage, question the evidence, and to see to it that no unproven case is given an affirmative decision. He also defends the rights of the other spouse. He is not really out to block your annulment, only to see that if it is granted, it is on solid legal grounds.

The Promoter of Justice   The Promoter of Justice is the defender of the public good. He makes sure that proper procedure is followed throughout the case and that no "public scandal" is given. These days, the office is usually combined with the office of the Defender of the Bond. Under the New Code, laypeople are being encouraged to serve as both Promoters of Justice and Defenders of the Bond.

The Advocate   This is your lawyer. It is possible that another Advocate will be appointed to defend your ex-spouse's rights if he or she insists, but usually there is only one Advocate and he is your representative in the case. Generally, the Advocate is a priest and canon lawyer, but may be a member of the laity. The Advocate helps you build your case, collect evidence, and get in touch with witnesses. He then argues your case before the Tribunal. Other sources may refer to this official as the Auditor or the Priest-Attorney. Even before the New Code went into effect, there were lay Advocates in some dioceses. I foresee the day when most Advocates will be lay people. Whatever the Advocate is called, he is on your side. In some dioceses, especially where the parish priest has helped you prepare the petition and gather the facts, you may never even meet your Advocate. He meets you only on paper.

A positive aspect of the New Code is that it encourages lay participation as Tribunal officials. If such lay participation is promoted to the fullest, the ultimate benefits would be immeasurable. If the priest canon lawyers could be saved from much of the drudgery and time-consuming aspects of the Tribunal work, they could concentrate on the judicial questions and general supervision of the Tribunals. But if there is an attempt to require canon law degrees of participating officials, then the laity will in fact be effectively shut out of real participation. If this develops, I think the American bishops may request an indult (special permission) for relief from such a burdensome restriction.

II. PRELIMINARY STEPS TOWARD AN ANNULMENT

Now that you know something about the Tribunal, it is time to examine the annulment procedure. Before approaching any Tribunal, however, you should see that two very important preliminary steps are out of the way. These steps are as follows:

A. Completion of Civil Divorce

No Tribunal will consider an annulment case before the parties have already received a divorce or civil annulment; the partners must have decided that there is no possibility of reconciliation. So if you haven't filed for a civil divorce or annulment yet, or if it is still in process, it must be finished before filing the petition for annulment.

B. Decide Which Tribunal to Approach

Before the APN went into effect, annulments were almost always granted by the Tribunal of the diocese of the husband. Then the APN came along and greatly increased the options. Under the APN you were allowed to petition for an annulment in your diocese; your former spouse's diocese; the diocese where the marriage took place; or any other forum where the proper proofs that the case could be best dealt with there could be presented, assuming certain consents were previously obtained. These may all have been the same diocese, of course, but it was worth knowing the options because, unfortunately, some Tribunals are more functional than others. Chicago, New York and San Diego, for example, have large staffs and process a large number of cases each year. At the other end of the spectrum are the Tribunals that have no full-time staff. According to a Canon Law Society of American survey several years ago, about 30 percent of the diocese tribunals were quite nonfunctional. The old nonfunctional dioceses have, for the most part, become much more active, but there is no denying that efficiency and openness to certain grounds varies widely from diocese to diocese. Cases that would easily result in a favorable ruling in some dioceses might be rejected or ruled upon unfavorably in others. Castelli describes this as "geographic morality," or what the Canon Law Society calls "divisive pluralism."

> On one level, this refers to the fact that some diocesan tribunals are better staffed and financed than others. But, more important, it refers to the fact that some dioceses refuse to grant annulments on the same grounds allowed in other dioceses.*

It is a sad fact that this "geographic morality" takes place, but forewarned is forearmed.

With the promulgation of the New Code came a step backward in the ability to exercise options in selecting a Tribunal. The old practice of "forum-shopping" has now been limited. The New Code provides that the petition may be filed in the diocese of the Petitioner only if the Petitioner's domicile is the same as the Respondent's. If the Petitioner's domicile is different, the petition must be filed in the domicile or quasi-domicile of the Respondent. The Petitioner can, however, have the case processed outside of the Respondent's domicile with the consent of the Tribunal of the respondent upon proper proof that, say, the Petitioner's domicile would be more appropriate. A proper proof might be, for example, that all the witnesses and most proofs exist in the Petitioner's domicile.

Although the Respondent has to be consulted about the re-

*Castelli, What the Church Is Doing, p. 31.

quested change in forum, he or she does not have a veto on the question. The Respondent's Tribunal makes the final decision. When this question was up for discussion in Rome, the American bishops generally favored a liberal approach to the question of forum choice. The wording of the New Code shows they were not entirely successful.

In determining whether to assume jurisdiction over a case where a Respondent lives elsewhere, an important concern is whether the assuming jurisdiction will be better able to provide pastoral care to the interested parties.

I believe that the granting of such requests for change in forum will in most cases become automatic, especially in the United States. The United States, with its extremely mobile population, would be faced with immensely greater administrative delays than other countries if a workable forum-switching mechanism does not evolve. In point of fact, form letters requesting such forum changes have already been proposed.

What if you have no idea where your former spouse lives? In such cases the Petitioner will be allowed to file in his or her own Tribunal. A good-faith effort must be made to locate the Respondent, though.

III. THE ANNULMENT PROCEDURE—PART 1

The following pages will give you an idea how your case will be handled. There are variations from diocese to diocese, however, and you may find certain steps combined in some places. But, generally speaking, you can expect to start off by making the initial contact and then completing the first form or interview.

Assuming your civil divorce is complete and you know which Tribunal to approach, making contact with the Tribunal is the first step you must take. It is at this very point that many remarried Catholics get cold feet. All kinds of fears rush in. Cold rejection as an unrepentant sinner is right up at the top of the list. If you are not yet remarried, it would be best to hold off remarrying until after your annulment has been granted. This indicates good faith and a willingness to abide by the Church's laws.

But if, like many divorced Catholics, you have long since remarried outside the Church, do not let that fact stop you from approaching the Tribunal. It is precisely for you that the Church has clarified the grounds for annulment and removed the excommunication penalty. Although still creaky, inconsistent, and rather difficult, today's annulment procedures are nevertheless much less rigid and harsh than the old laws. In following the annulment process, try to see the genuine pastoral concern of the Church officials who, like you, are caught up in the complicated machinery of canon law. They will do their best for you, but you must retain your patience (and often your sense of humor too). Do not overreact to requests. Let them guide you through the steps which, though they may seem archaic and burdensome, will nevertheless in most dioceses almost assure you of success. As you try to hold your patience, you should realize that those on the Tribunal are really trying to help you. For those of you who have had sad experiences in your civil divorces, things will really not seem so bad at all.

A. The Initial Contact

The Parish Priest You will usually begin by talking to your parish priest. Ideally, he will then contact the Tribunal for you. When the first papers arrive he will then assist you in filling them out. In many instances, such as in very busy or very small dioceses, your contact with the priest may constitute the first interview, and you will never have to talk with a Tribunal official at all. In some dioceses, the parish priests are trained to act as Advocates. Where this is the practice, it can produce a much warmer atmosphere, make for better communications regarding the progress of the case, and in general give you more confidence in your Advocate.

Going Directly to the Tribunal You may be confronted with a less than ideal relationship with your Advocate. And it is here that the point must be made: Each diocese is different. This book will tell you the general rules, procedures, and grounds. Such knowledge should greatly aid you as you travel the labyrinth of the annulment process in your diocese, but be prepared for a possible twist or turn peculiar to your diocese. The

New Code, in stressing the Principle of Subsidiarity, gives more and more administrative options to local dioceses. Many priests are as helpful as can be desired, but others may be uninformed, busy, or unsympathetic to your problem. Some may view your search for an annulment as a self-indulgent attempt to evade the just consequences of a marital breakdown for which you may be partly responsible. Others, especially in view of the changes in the New Code, may be unsure of the applicable canon law. Through ignorance, an overloaded work schedule, or a desire to avoid the whole issue, they may tell you that you have no case. As mentioned before, one woman of my acquaintance was discouraged by three different priests before she finally went on to petition for and receive her annulment. It is hard to be that persistent. Most parishioners think that they must accept their pastor's judgment on their case, and that if he says they have no grounds for an annulment they cannot proceed further. But keep in mind that he may well be uninformed in this specialized area of annulments. He may, in fact, be absolutely wrong, and you may still have open to you the next option I shall discuss.

If, for whatever reason, your parish priest is not helpful, you have a right to contact the office of the Tribunal directly. As a member of the Catholic Church, you have a right to present your petition before the proper authority and receive an acceptance or rejection for consideration of the petition. If, after reading this book, you feel you may have a case, then don't settle for anything less.

You will find the phone number of the Tribunal under the listings of the offices of the diocese, probably under "Office of the Tribunal." In smaller dioceses you may simply have to call the chancery office. When you call you will talk to a secretary, who will tell you the first steps in beginning the process in your diocese. The secretary will arrange for you to have an interview with someone from the Tribunal. If you have chosen this direct approach, you will want to make it clear that you wish to talk to the appropriate person about filing your petition directly with the Tribunal. Otherwise the secretary may shunt you aside with the suggestion that "you'll have to talk to your parish priest about that." When you take this direct approach, the office of the Tribunal will assign an Advocate to your case, and the Advocate will probably be the one who interviews you and continues to work closely with you throughout the case.

The hardest part about this stage is just getting started. It takes a real effort of will to stop by the rectory or pick up the phone and commit yourself. Whether you call on the parish priest or the Tribunal, your reluctance is understandable. But don't let fear overwhelm you! Visit the rectory or pick up that phone and dial! In a few months you may be very happy you had the guts to follow on through. Please forgive the pep talk, but I want to assure you that you have almost everything to gain and almost nothing to lose. Until now, more than 90 percent of divorced Catholics have failed to take advantage of their rights. Perhaps an awareness of those rights and the annulment procedures will encourage many to reconcile with the Church.

B. The First Form and Interview

Filling Out the First Form   Once you have contacted the Tribunal, whether through your parish priest or directly, you will have to fill out a form. The form will ask questions such as:

a. Are you baptized? When? Where?
b. Was your former spouse baptized?
c. When and where did your first marriage take place?
d. Has a civil divorce been obtained? When? Where? On what grounds?
e. Have you petitioned for annulment at any other Tribunal?

In addition, you will be asked why you think your first marriage was invalid. This may be a simple question calling for a long narrative statement or, alternately, a series of questions relating to the more common grounds. For example, the form may ask "Is there reason to believe that one or the other partner in the marriage never intended to be faithful?" Another question may be "Is there reason to believe that one or the other partner in the marriage never intended to have children?" In some dioceses, this form and the formal petition have been combined, thus eliminating a step and speeding up the process. In these dioceses, the form is much more elaborate and calls for a detailed statement about your entire relationship with your former spouse. In others, the questionnaire is quite simple and no detailed statement is required until later. But whatever way it is approached, the Tribunal is trying to determine two things: (1) Is it *procedurally* possible to process the petition? (2) Is there any indication that you have *grounds* for an annulment? A negative answer to either of these questions will stop the process right here. The procedural questions can be answered quickly. For basic jurisdictional purposes, the Tribunal needs to know if it has a right to hear your case. It must know, for example, if you can legally petition in this particular diocese. Thus it needs to know where you live and where your former spouse lives.

The questions about grounds, however, are ones of substance. The Tribunal must believe there is some reason to expect a favorable ruling on your petition before it will carry the process any further. It is at this point that some initial weeding out takes place. But don't worry; it is only the extremely weak cases that are dropped peremptorily. You have a very good chance of having your case accepted.

Further examples of the types of form questions you might have to answer are found in Appendix II.

The Interview   Somewhere along the line, you will be interviewed. This may merely be a discussion with your parish priest as you fill out the forms, or it may be an interview with an Advocate from the Tribunal. In dioceses where the first form is also a do-it-yourself petition, the interview may take place after you file your petition. But sooner or later you will talk to someone in detail about your case. That someone will be your parish priest if you start at the rectory, or possibly your Advocate if you start directly at the Tribunal. Most interviews take place at the parish rectory. The interviewers look for the answers to the same questions asked on the forms, and they do their best to help you come up with answers. This is one of the reasons why your chance of having your petition accepted is so good.

If, after a thorough discussion about your former marriage, your Advocate tells you you don't have a case, you can probably believe him. He is an expert on canon law and knows your chances before his diocese's Tribunal. It is much more likely, though, that your Advocate will tell you that you have a good chance of developing a favorable case, possibly on grounds you were unaware would apply or even existed. The whole purpose of the interview, from the Tribunal's point of view, is to get a handle on your situation and determine whether there are sufficient grounds in the case. If your Advocate is satisfied that it might be possible to establish a case for an annulment, he will go on, with the Tribunal's approval, to help process the petition.

Whether contact with your Advocate is frequent or rare (probably the latter), your Advocate is going to be your case's best friend in the months ahead. As a canon law expert, he may help you prepare your petition, and at the least, he will make sure it's in proper form. Your Advocate may help the Tribunal office contact witnesses, and may gather documents. He will ultimately prepare, or help prepare, a brief on your case and argue your cause before the judges of the Tribunal. He is your lawyer in the Church court.

Be aware, however, that there are certain differences between the role of an Advocate and that of a civil lawyer. A civil lawyer is expected to be one-sidedly in your favor—your hired legal gun, as it were. Although as an officer of the court your civil lawyer cannot misrepresent the facts, he can take an adversary position resolutely ignoring facts that might damage your case and leave the development of opposing facts to the other attorney. If the opposition isn't as well prepared, that is their tough luck. This is not the practice at the Marriage Tribunal. Your Advocate, though he will do everything possible to promote your case, must be much more evenhanded. The rather harsh adversary nature of civil law would be foreign to him. And don't ask him to wink an eye at awkward facts; he cannot do it. But those awkward facts may well be the facts that prove your marriage should be annulled. So be sure to tell your Advocate all the facts.

Of course another important distinction between the civil law hearings and canon law hearings is that the Tribunal can keep its eye on the ball. The canon law grounds for annulment can be carefully presented and examined without the myriad side issues that civil litigants must face. The Tribunal Judges do not have to concern themselves with who is awarded the imitation Ming vase purchased one-half by trading in the toaster given as a wedding present by John's Aunt Lucille and one-half with cash received from Mary's brother Bill. Bitter custody disputes do not have to be resolved. The most wrenching heartbreak is mostly over by the time the Tribunal rules. Skilled Tribunal officials can thus go right to the heart of the case before them.

IV. THE ANNULMENT PROCEDURE—PART 2

What You Send to the Tribunal

When the time comes to petition the Tribunal to hear your case, you may have a great deal of work to do. Again, it depends upon the diocese. Remember, however, that you have already overcome the first hurdle. The process is underway; you have had your interviews and you would not be encouraged to petition if there were not a good chance of your petition being granted.

A. The Petition and Statement

The petition form itself may arrive accompanied by work sheets and sample petitions that will help you get some idea of what the finished product should look like. The petition form will ask specific questions relating to various grounds. Most of these will require more than a yes or no answer. You will be asked to explain why you feel your marriage was invalid and on what grounds you think you are entitled to an annulment. Chapter 3 of this book will help you with these questions; your Advocate or parish priest will also help you.

You will also receive a request for a statement about your former marriage. You will be asked to review your courtship, engagement, honeymoon, married life, estrangment, separation, divorce, and current relationship with your former spouse in light of the grounds on which you are petitioning. Some people find this process therapeutic; others find it somewhat degrading. Mostly it is just hard work. When you have completed your statement, you may be required to have it no-tarized. Check your diocese's notary instructions carefully.

Here are some guidelines to help you in preparing your statement:

(1) Try to keep within the suggested space limit, which is usu-ally three to six pages.

(2) You will be asked for all details, but compliance with this is clearly impossible. Consult with your parish priest or Advo-cate and carefully follow his advice on what to include.

(3) Put the emphasis on your premarital relationship, engage-ment, and wedding day. With regard to postmarital facts, *be sure to point out problems that probably had their seeds in premarital causes.*

(4) Try to present your position cohesively and consistently. The Tribunal is not interested in your dredging up absolute-ly everything conceivable that your spouse has done wrong over the years. In the past, when Petitioners were so un-aware of the allowable grounds, this "shotgun" approach was used on the theory that possibly one or two pellets might hit the target.

If, for example, after talking with your parish priest or Advocate you feel that your grounds for annulment will be based on your ex-spouse's immature personality and alco-holism, you should concentrate your facts on these areas (although in truth the immature personality ground allows a great deal of diverse evidence).

B. Witness Information

Most formal annulment cases require three witnesses. This is part of the remaining difficulty in acquiring an annulment. It is not enough for you to know that your marriage was invalid; you must be able to prove it. Without witnesses, it is almost impossible to gain a favorable ruling. Keep in mind, however, that these witnesses do not have to know all the intimate de-tails of your marriage. They only have to be able to testify to those events or conversations which support that part of the case within their knowledge. These people can be relatives, friends, or professionals you have consulted, such as a marriage counselor. It is up to you, with your Advocate's aid, to contact your witnesses and gain their consent to testify. Usually they will not be asked to appear in person before the Tribunal. In most cases the Tribunal will send them a carefully worded questionnaire, asking only for information relative to the grounds upon which you are petitioning. Tribunals are much more willing to accept such written testimony than a civil court of law would be, where such writings might well be attacked as hearsay unless the opposition formally agrees in advance to allow the writings to be entered as evidence.

Sometimes a witness serves as little more than a character witness, verifying that you are a reliable individual who would tell the truth under oath.

Your major job at this point, then, is to find witnesses whose testimony will support your case, and then to notify them and obtain their consent to give such statements. Again, your Advocate will be of great help.

C. Necessary Documents

A surprising number of Church and civil documents must accompany your formal petition. The sooner you collect these, the better.

In most cases these will include:

(1) Copies of baptismal (and possibly confirmation) records on yourself.
(2) Civil and Church copies of the marriage license for your former marriage.
(3) A copy of the civil divorce decree (and possibly some of the proceedings). You probably already have a certified copy of your civil divorce decree, and a photocopy of this usually will suffice. If you don't have a copy, you can obtain one from the Clerk of Court where your divorce was granted.
(4) A signed, possibly notarized, release for any relevant medical or counseling records to be used in the case.

You will expedite the process if you supply current addresses for all your witnesses and your former spouse. Since the Tribunal is required to send interpellations (formal questions) to your former spouse, the sooner they are sent out, the faster your case will be decided. Don't forget to comply with your diocese's requirements for notarization before sending the statement in. If a notary is required, the notary does not have to read all the details of the statement; he or she merely acknowledges that you signed it before him or her as provided by law.

By the time you have done all these things, you may be a bit worn out. You will have filled out forms, written a long statement, chosen and contacted witnesses, and collected an array of documents. When you are finished, you may have a bulky package to give to the Tribunal. The filing fee for your petition is usually about $25.00.

Now you can relax. Almost all of your part of the work is done. From here on, the case will have a life of its own. You may be informed periodically about what stage the case has reached, but unless you are, say, asked to speak with a psychological expert because of the nature of your grounds, there is not much else to do now except exercise patience. In some dioceses you are notified in writing of the names of all the members of the court and are given a limited time period in which to file objections to anyone you want removed. Other dioceses only inform you of your Advocate's name; you never learn the identity of the others working on your case.

Optimally, the final decision should be handed down within about six months of the formal acceptance of your petition for consideration. Under the now-superseded APN, the decision was to be handed out within six months. Some Tribunals were able to meet this deadline, but most did not. Canon lawyers now almost unanimously say that there will at first be somewhat of a slowdown in the time taken to render decisions, at least until the sharp edges of the procedures of the New Code are worn down a bit.

In most cases you will not be officially notified when your petition has been accepted for consideration. Even if your petition is not accepted at this early stage you should not necessarily abandon your case. The reason for nonacceptance will be stated. Often you can refile a successful petition by merely supplying details omitted from your first petition. You will, however, be notified in writing when the final decision is made.

V. THE ANNULMENT PROCEDURE—PART 3

What Happens Inside the Tribunal

Strictly speaking, it is not essential for you to know any of this. You may be informed by letter or through your Advocate when various stages in the procedure have been reached, but that is only for your own information and peace of mind. There is nothing you must or, indeed, probably can do. Of course, if you are a person who can push matters to the back of your mind until you receive the final decision, so much the better. But if, like most people, you are curious about what is happening, the following will give you some idea just what is going on within the Tribunal while you wait.

A. Appointment of the Court

When all the papers of the formal petition are in order, a court will be appointed for your individual case. This means that people in at least three capacities will be working on your case at the Tribunal level. These court officials and no others will have exclusive jurisdiction over your case until the final verdict is rendered.

The Judges   As mentioned before, prior to the inception of the APN, a court was made up of three Judges as well as two Advocates. Norm #3 of the APN allowed cases to be heard by one Judge in situations where it was necessary. In practice, most Tribunals routinely determined that it was necessary. Norm #3 greatly increased the efficiency of the Tribunals, as it allowed, at least in theory, almost three times as many cases to be considered by the Judges as previously. But now the Great Experiment of the APN has ended and so has the one-judge option. The results: a longer annulment process and, in my opinion, a huge missed chance for the Church. But, as pointed out before, the authorization of more lay involvement in the Tribunals will serve to more than make up for this change if full advantage is taken of the authorization.

There are a couple of options still open to the Tribunal in fulfilling its judicial function. For example, some of the old efficiency may still be retained by assigning an individual judge to process each third case after all three have heard the evidence and voted on the decision. Because of the sheer weight of the ever-increasing annulment filings, some kind of option such as this will have to be implemented or the Tribunals will be buried in paper work.

The Defender of the Bond   As you will recall, the Defender of the Bond is the official who sees to it that the sanctity of marriage is upheld in the proceedings and that the rights of the other spouse are not violated. In modern Tribunals, the Defender of the Bond often also serves as the Promoter of Justice, and so has the additional job of making sure everything is done in accordance with overall justice. As I have intimated before, Petitioners may tend to see this individual as the villain of the piece, out to spoil their chance of an annulment by defending the existence of an already irrevocably broken marriage. In practice, the Defender of the Bond is unlikely to do more than require that the arguments in favor of the annulment be tightly and clearly presented. He may point out flaws in the case, attack certain auxiliary grounds as inaccurate, and in general keep your Advocate on his toes, but when it comes down to the final decision, he will not stand in your way if you have a valid case. In fact, Defenders of the Bond have regularly in the past exercised their right to waive appeal. Before the APN went into effect, the Defender of the Bond was required to appeal any decision granting annulment. In other words, any petition that was successful had to be heard twice. Norm #23 of the APN said that in cases where an appeal "against an affirmative decision would clearly be superfluous" the Defender of the Bond may be dispensed from the obligation to appeal. In practice, almost all appeals were dispensed with by Defenders of the Bond in most jurisdictions. The Pope became very concerned about this lack of annulment appeals in the United States, which is probably a major reason why the review requirement was reintroduced in the New Code. Even though a nonaffirmance of a Tribunal decision will be extremely rare, the additional review step burdens the annulment process with one more delay.

In any event, the local Defender of the Bond is truly not out to obstruct an annulment if one should be granted.

The Petitioner's Advocate The Petitioner's Advocate is the same person with whom, in many cases, you have been working all along. He is "your" canon lawyer, and has helped you at almost every step of the process so far. When the court is appointed, he is officially designated to represent your interests in the proceedings.

One More Form to Sign When you are notified that a court has been appointed, you will be asked to sign a form signifying your willingness to have this particular Advocate represent you at the trial. This is only a formality, but it must not be neglected. If, for example, you go on vacation for several weeks without signing the form, the court will probably do nothing until you get back. In some dioceses you sign this authorization at the same time that you sign the Petition, sometimes even as a part of the petition itself.

B. The First Session

After the court has been officially appointed for your case, it will set a date and have a first session. At this session it will be decided:

(1) Whether this Tribunal has jurisdiction over this case.
(2) Whether a preliminary showing of sufficient grounds has been presented.
(3) Whether sufficient sources of proof seem to be available.
(4) What the specific grounds seem to be in this case. Much of this may appear to you to be mere formality; the Tribunal makes a finding regarding matters that you and your Advocate investigated some time ago. If the answers to any of the first three questions were likely to be no, you probably would have been told so unofficially at an earlier stage. In most dioceses very few cases are thrown out at a First Session. Some winnowing has already taken place at the first interviews, and the First Session merely gets things down on paper officially and sets the stage for the next important step, the gathering of evidence.

If at the gathering of evidence your Advocate decides that

your case is hopeless, he'll usually lay the cards on the table and tell you what you're faced with. It is at this point that the second winnowing out of cases takes place. If they are faced with frank pessimism, Petitioners sometimes voluntarily abandon their cases. Some dioceses encourage this voluntary abandonment on extremely weak cases rather than have the petitioner go through the entire annulment procedure. It also often occurs at this point that someone within the Tribunal manages to see a new approach to a case that might otherwise be doomed to failure. Providing new information conforming to these new insights will sometimes save a case. In any event, as I have pointed out before, the large majority of cases will proceed on through to success.

C. The Court Gathers Evidence

Contacting Your Former Spouse The Tribunal must contact your former spouse, who must be told that an annulment procedure is underway and upon what grounds. The former spouse must then be given time to respond. If you have the address of your former spouse, it is in your own best interest to give this information to the Tribunal at the outset. Under the New Code, of course, the address of the spouse is needed not only for the sending of interpellations but also to determine if the case has been filed in the proper place. In the annulment proceedings you and your former spouse are usually referred to respectively as the Petitioner and the Respondent. In practice, Respondents usually do not "respond" at all. Occasionally they actively help the Petitioners, since if they are Catholic they are in the same dilemma as the Petitioners regarding their Church status. But even if you file the petition and your former spouse refuses to cooperate in any way, your case can still proceed, after the required waiting period of about a month. Even in the unlikely event that your divorced spouse opposes the whole case or the specific grounds you have selected, the case will continue. The Tribunal will hear any opposing evidence the former spouse wishes to present and even appoint an Advocate to defend his or her interests if the Respondent desires, but the case will be heard on the grounds you and your Advocate have selected, since you are the Petitioner.

Experience has shown that in most cases Respondents ignore the questions, or interpellations, sent to them, and in general are not too willing to put themselves out to help the Petitioner. Realistically, you should probably not rely too heavily on a former spouse's cooperation unless you have gained his or her consent to help beforehand.

Contacting the Witnesses   In most instances the witnesses are sent a carefully worded questionnaire that asks specific questions relating to the particular grounds you have selected. The witnesses are asked to complete this questionnaire and usually have it notarized before returning it to the Tribunal. In some dioceses, and for some cases, the witnesses are interviewed by the court.

Another Interview   It is possible that you may be asked to have an interview with a psychologist or psychiatrist who will later testify. This is most likely to be required if your petition is based on psychological grounds. Don't let this process frighten you if it is required. In fact, your own Advocate may suggest the need for such evidence. Psychological experts working with the Tribunals are likely to be very sympathetic to your situation. Their testimony often "makes" a case that might otherwise be difficult to prove.

Since Tribunals are swamped with paperwork these days, additional interviewing is kept to an absolute minimum. If a questionnaire will suffice, it will be used. Even though the percentage of divorced Catholics petitioning for annulments is extremely small, that small percentage represents, as we have already discussed, a quantum increase in numbers over those of a few years ago. It is probably a safe bet that, with further delays resulting from the New Code, there will be even fewer personal interviews with psychological experts than in the past.

An Outside Professional Opinion   It often occurs in psychological cases that the psychological expert does not personally interview you or appear at the trial. Instead, the evidence is collected and summarized, and then sent to the psychological expert. He or she studies it and then renders a written opinion.

This professional opinion is introduced as evidence when the case is finally heard.

These written report procedures are much more common than requiring the expert to give personal testimony.

Meanwhile, You Wait . . . The gathering of evidence is usually the most time-consuming part of the annulment process. It is impossible to say how long your case will take from beginning to end. If your former spouse cannot be located, if witnesses are slow to return the questionnaires, and if the psychological experts have difficulty finding time to attend to your case, it all adds to the time required. If you inquire about the progress of your case during this period, you will probably be told little except that evidence is being gathered. If a witness suddenly refuses to give a statement, or if there is a need for more information to build the case, the court will contact you. This is the time to be patient; you have not been forgotten. As a rule of thumb, allow four to six months from the time the court has been appointed before you inquire about the status of your case. Try to keep the process in perspective. Unless the time element is an all-consuming factor (for example, if you're holding off remarriage pending the Tribunal decision), remember: if your case is still being processed you will in all likelihood get your annulment (probably based on one of the new or expanded grounds). Of course if you have already remarried, the time factor may not be as pressing. Things are going your way.

D. The Final Hearing

Eventually the gathering of evidence is complete. When enough evidence has been collected, you may be notified through your Advocate or by letter that a date has been set for your final hearing, but in many dioceses you will have no idea when your case is actually heard. Even if you are notified of the hearing date, your presence will probably not be required. It is now rare for Petitioners to be present at the final hearing of their case.

The Defender of the Bond and your Advocate will both have prepared legal briefs presenting their positions. At the final hearing these will be delivered to the Judges, along with oral or additional written arguments. Usually the whole process is recorded so it can be later transcribed.

The Judges are required to reach "moral certainty" in their decisions. Moral certainty is more difficult to arrive at than being convinced of a "preponderence of evidence," which is required in most civil cases, but is less difficult than being convinced "beyond reasonable doubt," which is demanded in criminal trials.

If your case has proceeded this far, though, your chances of success are very good.

E. The Decision

The written decision of the Tribunal is the least impressive-looking document of the whole annulment process. It is usually just a short letter or small slip of paper that you receive in the mail one day. No fancy or multipaged document, the "sentence," or decision, informs you in the briefest terms whether your petition has been granted.

VI. THE ANNULMENT PROCEDURE—PART 4

Reviews and Appeals

When you receive the letter that officially informs you of the court's decision, it means that the "trial" is over. What follows next is a re-examination of the court's decision by someone else. One type of re-examination is required; the other is optional. This difference will be explained in the following paragraphs.

A. The Automatic Review

As we discussed earlier, the New Code has made an automatic review of each annulment proceeding mandatory. The vote on the canon requiring an automatic review passed by a vote of 46 to 13 at the Roman *plenarium*, in spite of attempts, led chiefly by the Americans, to modify it.

Such required review reflects the deep concern in Rome about the growing rate of annulments, but there is no turning back the clock. Tribunals are now generally all so dedicated to helping people gain annulments that there is little chance of one level working against the other. In practice, this automatic review may tend to slow down the annulment process, but most informed people are confident that the delay will not be significant. What it means for you is that it may take a little longer to receive the final approval of your annulment, but it will not materially affect your chances of receiving a favorable ruling.

You should also keep in mind that this new procedure will not be an "appeal to the Court of Second Instance," but rather merely the sending of the decision of the Court of First Instance to the Court of Second Instance for review. The Court of Second Instance will probably not ever "reverse" the decision of the Court of First Instance; instead it will either affirm the decision or require a retrial of the case. The main practical difference between a regular appeal to the Court of Second Instance and the automatic review is this: If you lose an appeal, there has been an adverse decision on the merits of your case and the case is over (except for the extremely rare Third Instance appeal). But if you lose an automatic review your case is still alive; it must, however, be retried at the First Instance level. And as mentioned before, the automatic review will almost always be decided in favor of the Petitioner.

So the so-called automatic appeal will be more toothless in practice than once feared. Still, the final decision is nonetheless delayed to some extent.

B. Your Right of Appeal

The Defender of the Bond is not the only one who may turn to the Court of Second Instance. If it should happen that you are not granted an annulment, you may appeal the decision to the Court of Second Instance.

An appeal by a Petitioner from an adverse decision is, for several reasons, a very rare occurrence today. First, in many dioceses, more than nine out of ten people whose petition proceeds to final decision receive an annulment. Second, virtually all those who have no chance of proving their case are advised to drop the proceedings before the Final Hearing is reached.

Third, those who cannot prove their case before the Tribunal usually fall back on the Internal Forum, rather than pursue the case in another court. But on the off chance that you may wish to appeal an adverse decision, a brief explanation of the appeal system follows.

The Court of Second Instance   The Tribunal will inform you that your petition for annulment has been denied and tell you where you may appeal. The Appeals Tribunal (the Court of Second Instance) is usually in a neighboring diocese.

It is up to you to contact the Appeals Tribunal. An appeal or review on your behalf does not automatically take place if you lose your annulment case, but only if you win it and the annulment has been granted. Once you have notified the Appeals Tribunal, someone from the Appeals Tribunal will get in touch with the first Tribunal and have all the information on the case forwarded. You will now be dealing exclusively with the Appeals Tribunal. (Talk to your local First Instance Tribunal officials about the mechanics of your diocese's appeal.)

The Appeals Tribunal will meet, often within a month, to bring things together in what is called "the joining of the issues." Was the proper ground for decision used by Judges in the Court of First Instance? Was there sufficient evidence to justify the decision? Were any issues overlooked or given undue consideration?

At that time, you or the court may request further investigation, or it may be decided to simply review the first court's decision on the basis of existing evidence. In the Court of Second Instance, a decision ideally should take no more than one month, but is usually takes longer.

Only 855 Second Instance decisions were handed down in 1981 in the United States.

The Court of Third Instance   The Rota at Rome is called the Court of Third Instance and, theoretically, a final appeal can be made to this body. This process is so rare and complicated that it falls outside the scope of this book. If you have lost twice in the liberal American Tribunals, an appeal to Rome would probably be futile. In 1981 only seven decisions were made by the Court of Third Instance on United States' appeals.

3

The Selection of Grounds and the Rise of the Psychological Cases

Let's assume that you have decided to petition for an annulment. It will be tremendously beneficial to you to understand the limited, formal grounds upon which a decree of nullity can be granted. This way you can decide how the facts of your particular situation fit the requirements of canon law.

Some divorced people shy away from attempting to pigeonhole the reasons for their marital breakup into a ready-made category. It seems too cold and impersonal. But, on the other hand, since you have already gone through a civil divorce, you may understand why this procedure is necessary. No matter what you may have told yourself and your family about the reasons for your civil divorce, when you approached the civil court it was necessary to put it into formal language and you were granted a divorce based on specific legal grounds. In nofault states it would have been based on an irretrievable breakdown of the marriage, regardless of whose fault it was; in other states it would have been based on grounds such as cruel and inhuman treatment, mental cruelty, adultery, desertion, commission of a felony, or chronic alcoholism. This is the language of the civil divorce courts, and you were forced to fit your own personal and unique case into this language before the state could grant you a divorce.

Similarly, the Diocesan Marriage Tribunal that we have been discussing is also a court of law, and must approach your case within its own legal structure and formal terminology. It can deal with your problem in no other way. Your Advocate, of course, is highly skilled in these matters. But it will help you immensely if you have some grasp of the options and are able to discuss them intelligently.

There is very little written in this area for the layperson or the expert, and what is available to the expert is written in language so obscure that even an expert is hard pressed to understand it. Even the experts are inconsistent in their language and often argue about interpretations. With the adoption of the New Code it will be even harder for some time to get authoritative statements from Church officials about many of these matters. To help remedy this situation, this chapter gives a simplified presentation of some of the most common and fruitful grounds, arranged by the three major types of cases and their most important subcategories. A grasp of this structure should be all that is necessary to be well informed about the selection of grounds.

THREE TYPES OF CASES

Cases presented to the Tribunal will generally fall into one of these three types:

(1) Formal Cases of Annulment. In these cases it is legally proven that no valid sacramental union ever took place. A formal case requires a full Tribunal procedure and is the most common type. Almost all cases involving a typical Catholic marriage will fall into this category.

(2) Documentary Cases. These are cases in which some formal bar to marriage can be easily documented, such as where a proper ceremony was not followed. These are usually cases involving an interfaith (referred to as "mixed" in the canons) marriage or a marriage of Catholics "outside the Church," or where the circumstances surrounding the wedding ceremony itself were highly unusual.

(3) Privilege or Dissolution Cases. These are the oldest grounds for ending a marriage bond and could be said to be Catholic divorces, or dissolutions, rather than annulments. They are of most use to recent converts who have previous

non-Catholic marriages, and to Catholics formerly married to unbaptized (as opposed to merely non-Catholic) spouses.

I. FORMAL CASES OF ANNULMENT

Most petitions that reach the Tribunal are formal cases of annulment. This is because a properly performed and consummated marriage between two living Roman Catholics can only be nullified by the formal annulment process. Since a valid sacramental marriage can never be *dissolved*, a successful Petitioner must prove that it never really existed in the first place. It requires a full tribunal procedure with a Court selection and a formal hearing, as discussed in the last chapter. In 1981 there were 58,475 reported formal annulment petitions filed in the United States. Appendix III shows a diocese-by-diocese filing of formal petitions.

There are many canon law grounds upon which a civilly failed marriage might be declared null, but most of them are exceedingly difficult to prove. For most practical purposes, the usable grounds for formal annulment can be divided into three important subcategories: the new psychological grounds, total or partial simulation of consent, and force and fear. Almost all formal annulment cases in the United States today make use of one or a combination of the above three subcategories in one way or another.

A. The New Psychological Grounds

The importance of the adoption of psychological grounds for annulment is incalculable. Without a doubt, these new grounds are the most fruitful approach open to the average Catholic seeking a formal annulment. Statistics indicate that over 80 percent of all formal annulments granted in the United States in the past ten years have been based on psychological grounds. I have mentioned several ways in which the New Code has slowed down the annulment process, at least in the United States. But those in favor of easing the annulment process can claim one gigantic victory in the adoption of these new grounds.

Use of the "psychological" grounds was not only not obstructed, as had been feared, but the grounds were actually written into the New Code! In countries other than the United States (which have been much more hesitant to use psychological grounds), a whole new approach to annulment now exists. The American experience will prove invaluable to the rest of the Church in this area.

Although one faction in Rome pressed strongly for the elimination of the psychological grounds in the proposals for the New Code, Fr. Navarette of Georgian University argued very strongly for keeping these grounds. If the psychological grounds had in fact been eliminated from the New Code, the heart would have been cut out of annulment rights within the Church and far fewer Catholics would be able to obtain formal annulments.

The Old Code and The New Psychological Grounds   The new psychological grounds have grown out of a developing interpretation of the Old Code's concern with defective matrimonial consent. While the Code of Canon Law of 1917 does not speak directly about psychological incapacity, such grounds have long been deduced from a combination of three old canons: Canon #1081 required persons to be "capable according to law" in order to give valid consent; Canon #1082 required that persons "be at least not ignorant" of the major elements required in marriage; and Canon #1087 (the force and fear category) required that internal and external freedom be present in order for consent to be valid.* This line of interpretation produced two distinct but related grounds for annulment, called "lack of due discretion" and "lack of due competence." Lack of due discretion means that the person did not have the *ability to give valid consent at the time* of the wedding and therefore the union is invalid. Lack of due competence means that the person was *incapable of carrying out the obligations* of the promise he or she made during the wedding ceremony.

The New Code and the New Grounds   There was concern in the past that the New Code of Canon Law would repudiate these interpretations, tightening up the canons so as to exclude psy-

*Hudson, Handbook II, p. 185.

chological grounds. As mentioned before, what in fact happened was just the opposite: The New Code formally adopts the psychological grounds presently being used; it makes them explicit. According to Canon #1095 of the New Code, the following are incapable of contracting marriage: (1) those who lack sufficient use of reason (to be distinguished from mental illness, which is considered in the next category); (2) those who lack judgmental discretion concerning the matrimonial rights and duties to be mutually handed over and accepted; (3) those who, due to a serious psychic anomaly, cannot assume the essential obligations of matrimony.

By codifying these grounds, particularly lack of due discretion and lack of due competence, the Church has done itself and its members inestimable good. As we have discussed, the American Tribunals had been using these psychological grounds for almost a decade before enactment of the New Code. Thus, even though some of the efficient American *procedures* are at least temporarily superseded, the fact that psychological *grounds* for nullity were retained is all-important. With those grounds, used alone or perhaps with others, you will probably be able to obtain a formal annulment if your irretrievably broken marriage has been dissolved by the civil courts.

It is clear that there is no intent in the New Code to block annulments based on these tremendously important grounds. The New Code not only expands the old categories, but actually creates new categories for annulment based on the advances made in psychology during the past century.

A Change in the Nature of Evidence Use of the new psychological grounds as set forth in the New Code has been coupled with a new interpretation of relevant evidence in annulment cases. The difficulty in annulment cases has always been the necessity of proving the existence of any invalidating impediment at the time of the ceremony. 1970 is often thought of as ushering in a new era in Tribunal practice, primarily because of the beginning of the APN and because of the fact that the first use of the psychological grounds came shortly thereafter. But even before 1970, the winds of change had been blowing for a new approach to examination of psychological evidence. Favorable annulment decisions by the Roman Rota in the

1950s and 1960s involving sexual disorders such as homosexuality and nymphomania laid the foundation for a broader approach to the kind of proof necessary for psychological grounds for annulment. The Rota had reasoned for the first time in several cases that the capacity to give valid consent *at the time of* marriage was probably not present in persons who had displayed such problems shortly *after* the marriage. The nature of this change was nothing short of revolutionary. Once the Rota itself had demonstrated a cautious willingness to use this kind of hindsight, the way was paved for what came after 1970. Diocesan Tribunals began to accept proof of serious psychological problems that manifested themselves shortly *after* the ceremony as proof of an inability to give valid consent *at the time of* the ceremony.

Furthermore, and equally significant, the professional opinion of a psychological expert became increasingly important in such cases. Data about the person's entire life, both before and after the ceremony, were presented to these experts and they were asked to give professional opinions about a party's mental capacity at the time of the wedding. These opinions were rarely challenged and tended to be accepted as decisive evidence of lack of valid consent.

The Church took pains to point out that its new openness in this area did not amount to the addition of new grounds for annulment, but rather was an accommodation by the Church to the advances made in psychology during the past decades. There was now the expertise to provide the all-important connecting link between a marriage breakdown and premarital causes.

The Evolving Concept of Marriage   During the 1970s the Church broadened its whole idea of marriage from that of a legal contract to that of a covenant. The result of this was that it could no longer be assumed in annulment cases that a person who could intellectually understand the concept of marriage could necessarily give valid consent to marry. The ability to both grasp and assume the real obligations of a mature, lifelong commitment are now considered a necessary prerequisite to valid matrimonial consent.

The Resulting Explosion in the Number of Psychological Cases   As can be seen from the foregoing paragraphs, it has now become much easier to prove on psychological grounds that a sacramental union never took place. The result has been a mushrooming of petitions in this category as many Advocates advise Petitioners to take this approach. Psychological grounds are much the easiest to prove, even when more traditional grounds for petitioning may exist. Let's look at two hypothetical situations where this might be the case:

Example One   A man who was pressured by an overbearing father into "doing the right thing" at age 17 and marrying his pregnant girlfriend could have a difficult time proving that the force used on him was enough to warrant a decree of annulment based on Force and Fear grounds. But it would not be at all difficult to demonstrate that he was immature at the time, and that the pressure might well have deprived him of the ability to decide rationally about marriage. Evidence and testimony of immature behavior before and after the marriage, coupled with corroborative testimony by a psychological expert to the effect that the boy likely could not have fully appreciated the obligations of marriage under the circumstances, would be all that would be necessary to prove lack of due discretion in many Tribunals.

Example Two   Similarly, a woman attempting to gain an annulment on the ground of Intention Against Indissolubility (a popular subcategory of the Simulation of Consent category), would have to prove that her husband's intention to divorce was a consciously held reservation that existed prior to the ceremony, and not a later change of attitude. Even his own sworn testimony might not be sufficient evidence unless it were upheld by other proofs. But proof of the man's extramarital affairs, and a wide variety of other evidence, ranging from difficulty holding a job to trouble with the police, could be seen by a psychiatrist as indications of an antisocial personality (sociopathy), which would preclude the possibility of understanding or carrying out the obligations of a lifelong relationship. In this context, the husband's intention to divorce if he felt like it, regardless of when he came to this conclusion, would be seen as one more strong piece of evidence that he had always suffered from a psychological condition that made it impossible for him to "assume the essential obligations of matrimony." In this case the Advocate would probably advise a petition on psychological grounds, seeking a decree of annulment based on lack of due competence.

It is small wonder that the use of psychological grounds for annulment has grown to such proportions in recent years. As Sheed says,

> Many people believe virtually any failed marriage can be annulled on the basis of incapacity and immaturity. It is not all that difficult to prove that someone was immature at the time of marriage or did not fully understand all the obligations and developments involved in a lifelong marriage.*

It has been remarked facetiously that the Church would have even fewer priests if ordinations were subjected to similar hindsight psychological examinations. But to say this is to miss the point: No one is out to attack the validity of working marriages. Annulments are only sought by divorced Catholics who very much want to return to their Church and the sacraments. If the new psychological grounds have made this easier to do, so much the better for everyone.

Recognizing Grounds for a Psychological Case

The diagnosis of psychological problems is probably beyond any of us who are not psychological experts. But it is nevertheless possible to examine telltale signs in your former marriage that could indicate the presence of such problems. Of course if you or your spouse were ever treated for mental illness, such as schizophrenia, medical records of this sort would be very useful in an annulment case. But even without the presence of such serious problems, there are signs that might be indicators of problems. For example:

Epilepsy If either of you is epileptic and had an attack close to

*Sheed, Nullity of Marriage, p. 29.

the time of the ceremony, you may be able to prove lack of due discretion.

Intoxication   If one of you was intoxicated by alcohol or by a drug at the time of the ceremony, you may have a lack of due discretion case.

Alcoholism or Drug Addiction   This is a chronic condition that can be verified medically. If it existed shortly after the wedding, it may well have been there at the time you married.

Homosexuality   This is a condition that the Roman Rota accepts as proof of invalid consent at the time of the ceremony.

Immaturity   This is a very loose category. Look for some of the following at the time of the wedding: financial irresponsibility; refusal to take care of home or children; excessive dependence on, or rebellion from, parents; excessive reliance on peer approval; problem drinking; trouble with police or others in authority; difficulty in holding a job; extramarital affairs; or emotional instability.

In an article in *Catholic Mind*, Fr. Green lists six elements necessary to the mature marital relationship:

> The courts consider the following elements crucial to the marital commitment: (1) a permanent and faithful commitment to the marriage partner; (2) openness to children and partner; (3) stability; (4) emotional maturity; (5) financial responsibility; (6) an ability to cope with the ordinary stresses and strains of marriage, etc.*

Fr. Green goes on to speak about some of the psychological conditions that might lead to the failure of a marriage:

> At stake is a type of constitutional impairment precluding conjugal communion even with the best intentions of the parties. Among the psychic factors possibly giving rise to his or her inability to fulfill marital obligations are the following: (1) antisocial personality with its fundamental lack of

---

* Green, Catholic Mind, p. 49.

loyalty to persons or sense of moral values; (2) hyperesthesia, where the individual has no real freedom of sexual choice; (3) the inadequate personality where personal responses consistently fall short of reasonable expectations.*

Reasons Why the Psychological Grounds of Lack of Due Discretion and Lack of Due Competence Are the Most Popular Annulment Grounds Today

They Are New There is a very brief legal history of the use of lack of due discretion and lack of due competence, and all the precedent available comes from post-1970, which is very progressive in its interpretation. The intricacies involved in following the precedents of some of the other older categories are thus avoided.

They Are Easier to Prove With Tribunals now able to accept conduct after the ceremony as a strong indication of the psychological state of the partners at the time of the ceremony, one of the major stumbling blocks to an annulment is gone. Similarly, a wide array of evidence of behavioral patterns and examples of instability can now be brought into the case. Although no one of these alone could constitute evidence of invalidity, when collected and analyzed by a psychological expert they may well show the presence of a psychological state that would invalidate the marriage vows.

The use of psychological grounds for annulment is comparable to the use of the ground of mental cruelty, which is employed in civil divorce cases in states that still require proof of fault. Almost everyone who obtains a divorce in these states bases his or her case on the ground of mental cruelty even though a reason such as adultery or chronic alcoholism may be more to the point. It is much less traumatic for all involved to simply use these problems as examples of an overall problem than to try to dig out the sordid details of every affair or drinking binge and build a case revolving on the narrower, more specific ground.

* *Ibid.*

They Are Difficult to Challenge   Psychological cases rely heavily on testimony from psychological experts. Since the judges on the Tribunal are unlikely to have such extensive psychological training, they must give strong weight to expert testimony. If an expert says that one of the parties was incapable of making or keeping a marriage vow, the Tribunal is unlikely to question his or her opinion. That opinion, when received as evidence in the annulment case, becomes nearly unchallengeable proof of an invalid union.

They Are Broadly Applicable   The psychological grounds are the best approach for anyone who doubts whether he or she has a case for an annulment on any other terms. A situation that does into fit into any of the more traditional categories often fits very easily into the psychological category.

As new as the psychological grounds are, experts are already detecting a shift in their use. Whereas originally the emphasis was on the parties' inability to exercise proper judgment at the time of the marriage (lack of due discretion), recent cases seem to be concentrating on the parties' incapacity to assume or carry out their responsibilities and obligations as promised (lack of due competence). An advantage to using the ground of lack of due competence is that the civil divorce and breakup of the family almost always is proof of someone's failure to carry out marital responsibilities as promised at the time the marriage was entered into.

Those seeking an annulment should seriously consider the possibility of making use of the psychological category. Of all options in formal annulment cases, it is certainly the most promising.

B. Simulation of Consent

After the psychological grounds, probably the most fruitful grounds are those of total or partial simulation of consent. Consent to a marriage must not only be psychologically possible, it must be wholehearted. Any positive, conscious intention to make the consent conditional, or to exclude anything considered vital to a sacramental marriage, invalidates the union. The word *simulation* is not found in the canons, but it is commonly used in reference to any case in which the marital promises were only pretended, or simulated.

Canon 1101(2) of the New Code reads:

> If, however, either or both of the parties should by a positive act of will exclude marriage itself or any essential element of marriage or any essential property, such party contracts invalidly.

Total Simulation of Consent   Total simulation of consent occurs when one or both parties go through the outward forms of a wedding without any intention of really marrying. In other words, the ceremony takes place and all the witnesses and friends in attendance undoubtedly believe the couple intends to live happily ever after. Either or both of the parties, though, know they were just going through the motions. For some reason, they're faking it when they say "I do." This is rare, but sometimes happens to please a parent, to give a child a name, or perhaps to avoid the draft. Proof of strong motivation for simulating marriage is necessary, and substantial evidence of a complete lack of intention both before and after the ceremony to take the marriage seriously is needed.

Partial Simulation of Consent: Exclusion of any essential part of marriage also invalidates the marriage. A person who is willing to marry but at the same time consciously reserves consent to certain elements of the relationship engages in partial simulation. The most important of such reservations are intention against fidelity, intention against indissolubility, and intention against children. These are so frequently used that they are referred to as the "big three."* Tribunals receive many petitions each year based on charges of partial simulation in one of these three categories.

(1) Intention against fidelity. Fidelity means faithfulness, and an intention against it means one or both partners had no intention of giving the other exclusive sexual rights. Remember that this does not simply mean unfaithfulness during marriage. It is necessary to prove that the original promise of faithfulness was made insincerely. A man who had a lover at the

*Tierney, Annulment, p. 72.

time of his wedding whom he had every intention of continuing to see, or a woman who had a series of lovers during her engagement as well as after her marriage, would probably be considered to have invalidated their marriages by an intention against fidelity.*

(2) Intention against indissolubility. Also called intention against perpetuity, intention against indissolubility means that one or both partners reserved the option to divorce if things did not work out between them. This attitude is widespread in America today. There is not one mainline Protestant denomination that does not allow divorce and remarriage, though most do frown on it. The secular world is even more permissive, sometimes actively encouraging divorce rather than suggesting enduring marital difficulties. It would be very hard for American Catholics to remain uninfluenced by this prevailing cultural attitude. As we discussed in the first chapter, Catholics seem to have come to accept the reality of divorce. Although most Catholics still say they believe in the sanctity and indissolubility of marriage, they are now voting with their feet on the way to the doors of civil divorce courts, and are now divorcing at the same rate as the rest of the population. The Church, however, has not changed its stand on indissolubility. Marriage is still seen as a lifelong union and, ironically, any other attitude invalidates a marriage from the start.

Despite precana conferences, many young Catholics who know full well the Church's teaching nevertheless enter marriage with the conscious intention of reserving an option to divorce. The difficulty in proving this before a Tribunal is in establishing that this was an attitude that existed prior to the marriage and was not a later change of heart. As with the intention against fidelity, it is not the divorce per se, but rather the *intention to enter marriage while reserving the option to divorce* that allows the union to be annulled.

According to *People* magazine,** couples in Europe often write letters to a notary before the wedding declaring that they have no plan for a lifelong marriage. If trouble develops in their relationship, they can then use their letters as proof for annulment on the ground of intention against indissolubility. If

---

* Handbook, p. 155.
** People, July 28, 1980, p. 31.

an Advocate is looking for proof to annul a marriage based on an intention against indissolubility, he could hardly find better evidence to make a case. It does seem like a lousy way to start a marriage, though.

The Church's strong position on indissolubility is thus both a hindrance and a blessing to some. Although it is a hindrance to those wanting to remarry within the Church, the position is so absolute that, paradoxically, the marriage celebrants who do not embrace it fully can, as a result, have their marriages annulled.

(3) Intention against children. Since the Church teaches that a primary end of marriage is the procreation of children, any intention on the part of one or both parties to exclude children constitutes a ground for annulment. The Old Code specifically mentioned the conjugal rights of the spouse, while the New Code appears to include them under the phrase "essential element of marriage." But whichever Code is consulted, this intention centers on a refusal to allow intercourse to have its natural result.

Proving intention against children is not simply a matter, however, of proving the continued use of birth control, even artificial birth control. There must be real reason to believe that the intention was meant to be permanent or would have the natural effect of permanency. At least one of the partners believed there were to be no children, ever. The proof and argumentation of such cases is highly complex, but the essence of the argument is usually that there was a mutual or one-sided declared intention to use birth control for a certain length of time, which kept being extended as the marriage got worse and worse. Believable motives for such reservations are very helpful in proving such a case. If it can be shown, for example, that the woman has an excessive fear of pregnancy or the man an overly strong attachment to material possessions, it could help the case tremendously.

Problems with Simulation Petitions   The problems with simulation petitions are twofold. To begin, the first part of Canon #1101 reads:

> The internal consent of the mind is presumed to conform to
> the words or the signs used in the celebration of marriage.

In other words, the presumption is heavily on the side of validity. To succeed with such a petition, there must be strong proof
that what was promised was done so with a conscious intention of not following through. Secondly, it must be clearly demonstrated that this attitude was held at the time of the wedding
and was not a later change of attitude.

In most cases you will need:

(1) The judicial confession of the simulator—i.e., it must be
admitted to the Court.

(2) Witnesses to similar statements made outside of the Court,
especially before the marriage. A judicial confession is naturally
suspect, especially if made by the Petitioner.

(3) Indication of a strong motivation for simulating. People
just don't make false promises unless they have a reason for doing so.

So if you are considering a formal annulment, you should
carefully examine the main three grounds of simulation of
consent, even though simulation cases are not the easiest to
prove. The nature of the evidence necessary in any given case
obviously will differ. Your Advocate is, of course, the person to
consult on this. If you think you have a case on one of these
grounds do not hesitate to suggest it, especially if you think you
could use it in conjunction with other grounds.

C. Force and Fear

The Old Code One of the conditions of valid consent is that
the consent be freely given. The presence of actual force or real
fear of harm invalidates the marriage. Under the Old Code,
this category was intended to apply to such situations as politi-
cal or business marriages forced on the young people by their
parents, and, of course, the classic backwoods "shotgun wedding." In recent years the interpretation of this ground expanded so much that it was also used in cases merely involving premarital pregnancy. Advocates set out to prove that the heavy
social pressure exerted on couples in such a situation at least
potentially invalidated such marriages. The difficulty lay in

the fact that the Old Code required that the fear not only be grave but that the force be unjust. This concept is clear enough in the matter of a literal shotgun wedding, but attempting to define *unjust* in other contexts led to a great deal of speculation and legal interpretation.

An example of a marriage that might be annulled because of grave fear and unjust force is a case of a teenage girl who was told, and sincerely believed, that she would be turned out of her parents' home if she did not marry. This would be a grave fear and unjust force that would invalidate her marriage if she could prove it. In practice, what is happening more and more is that the Tribunals side-step the difficult question of grave fear and unjust force by focusing mostly on the emotional state of the partners. In other words, these cases become psychological cases judged under the more open ground of lack of due discretion. The Tribunals are operating on the (correct) assumption that it is much easier to prove one's own state of mind than to struggle with the intricacies of the definitions of force and fear in canon law.*

The New Code   The New Code changes some of this. Canon #1103 states that a marriage is invalid if it is entered into due to force or grave fear inflicted from outside the person, even when inflicted unintentionally, which is of such a type that the person is compelled to choose matrimony in order to be freed from it.

It is noteworthy that the old stipulation that the force be unjust is omitted in the New Code. The results could be far-reaching.

> The practical implication of this is that even a just fear inspired from without may in the future be considered as a possible cause of nullity of marriage: for example, a young girl becomes pregnant and chooses marriage because she fears the just displeasure of her parents.**

---

*Regarding the example given, that of teenage pregnancy, experience has shown that teenage marriages are suffering a 50 percent divorce rate, and the marriages involving premarital pregnancies are presently sustaining a substantially higher failure rate than that.
**Hudson, Handbook II, p. 123.

If this interpretation is adopted by the Tribunals, there may be a rapid increase in the use of force and fear as a ground for annulment. This is another change in canon law under the New Code, then, in which there has been movement toward the freer granting of annulments.

But a future Petitioner seeking annulment based upon force or grave fear will not necessarily have clear sailing even without the word "unjust." The fact that the new law still requires that the fear be grave and that it be inflicted from outside the person means that careful proofs are required to make an acceptable case. In the situation just quoted, for example, the young woman might still have trouble proving that there was reason for grave fear, regardless of whether it was justly or unjustly inflicted. Similarly, a young man who convinced himself that his girlfriend's father would kill him if he didn't marry her, when the father had done nothing to inspire such fear, may still have trouble because of the phrase "inflicted from outside the person."

The foregoing cautions are not intended to discourage use of the force and fear ground. You should simply be on notice that the proof required is substantial. In any case involving premarital pregnancy, however, it is probably a good additional ground to petition on, along with a psychological ground (which will probably be your main emphasis) in a formal petition for annulment.

Remember that in a petition for annulment based on force and fear:

(1) The fear must be "grave."
(2) The fear must be inspired from "outside," which means that it must be caused by someone other than yourself.
(3) The fear probably no longer need be "unjust" in its application or severity under the New Code.

To summarize regarding the formal cases for annulment, then: The new psychological grounds are by far the most widely used and are, in large part, accountable for the recent huge increase in annulments. Simulation of consent, especially the Big Three, can be applied in many cases, and the ground of force and fear, even though fairly rigid, still will be able to be applied quite often. Your chances of obtaining an annulment are best if you base your case on a psychological ground, but you may wish to bolster your case by also employing the grounds of simulation of consent or force and fear.

The New Code has ensured that the psychological grounds will be a mainstay in formal cases for annulment. The door has been permanently opened.

II. DOCUMENTARY CASES FOR ANNULMENT

A. Defect of Form

The Catholic Church has a strict set of requirements for the proper form of marriage. Except under special circumstances, Catholics must be married in the presence of a priest and at least two witnesses. That means, for example, that a civil marriage before a justice of the peace is not valid in the eyes of the Church if one of the partners is a Catholic.

Until recently, this was the rule for interfaith marriages as well. Now, however, with the permission of a bishop, a valid interfaith marriage may take place before a non-Catholic minister. The emphasis is now placed on the couple themselves and their promises to each other; these are the important elements in the sacrament, rather than on the officiating clergy.

Certain procedures must still be followed, however. If your marriage was not performed by a Roman Catholic priest, there is a good possibility that you may be able to acquire an annulment on the ground of defect of form. Documentary evidence proving that some element of the required form was missing, such as the presence of two witnesses or a bishop's permission for a non-Church wedding, is all that is needed for an affirmative decision. As a result, the decision can be made at the local level without going through the formal annulment process. No Court need be convened, no argument need be heard, no decision need be weighed, and usually no contested facts need be proven, so the time and expense involved are minimal.

Obtaining the official documents is the key to this type of annulment. Marriage certificates that show an improper officiating individual, or that show that two witnesses were not present, are submitted to the Tribunal. Without these, the case must be presented before a Court for decision, much like a petition for formal annulment.

Note that the ground of defect of form does not apply to non-Catholic marriages. The Church recognizes the validity of other forms of marriage in the case of non-Catholics. It is only the Catholic laity that is bound to observe proper canonical form or acquire the proper dispensation before marrying. Thus two Protestants married before a Protestant minister are validly married in the eyes of the Catholic Church, whereas two Catholics or a Protestant and a Catholic who have not obtained proper permission and who marry before someone other than a priest are not considered validly married. So a person who converted to Catholicism after marriage to a non-Catholic may not seek an annulment based on defect of form.

Since the appearance of the encyclical *Matrimonia Mixta* in 1970, couples entering interfaith marriages have a wider choice of ceremonies. Consequently, it is now possible for an interfaith marriage to take place with almost any appropriate ceremony, religious or civil, provided that permission of the bishop has been obtained. The result of this change might be a future decline in the number of annulments granted based on defect of form, but presently the number of petitions based on defect of form is increasing. The important thing to keep in mind is that despite the new freedom in interfaith marriages, permission of the bishop is still necessary. If you married in other than a Catholic ceremony before 1970, you probably did not obtain such permission. Even if your non-Catholic ceremony took place since that time, it is quite possible that permission was not obtained. It is worth checking if you are not sure.

It is no secret that many priests today practically counsel high-risk couples to marry outside the Church, thus preserving annulment grounds if they obtain a civil divorce. If the marriage works out, the couple can always regularize it within the Church.

Recent studies show that the U.S. Tribunals alone grant an astounding 85 percent or more of the defect of form annulments throughout the entire world. In 1981, about 24,000 annulment decisions based on defect of form were handed down in the United States.

B. Previous Bond

A Catholic with a previous valid marriage may not contract another marriage during the lifetime of the first spouse. It is precisely this rule that presents the problem for the divorced and remarried Catholic. Regardless of any civil divorce procedure, the Church insists that the first union is binding and refuses to allow another unless the first is annulled by the Marriage Tribunal. There are certain cases, however, where this "prior bond" rule can be used to the advantage of the Petitioner.

Especially for the convert or the Catholic who entered into an interfaith marriage, there is the possibility that your former spouse had been previously married before you married him or her. If it can be proven through official documents that your former spouse had entered into a valid marriage prior to marrying you, your own marriage to that person becomes invalid.

This can also be applied in your own case. For example, if you were a non-Catholic who was validly married in a non-Catholic ceremony and you later divorced, remarried, and then wished to become a Roman Catholic and have your present marriage recognized by the Church, it would be well to look into the whereabouts of your first spouse. The fact that your first marriage resulted in a valid bond would probably make any subsequent marriage invalid; and if your first spouse has died, your current marriage may be valid already or can quickly be made so.

The evidentiary requirement in previous bond cases is the irrefutable documentation of a previous marriage. If the proper documentation is available, the process does not require the convening of a Court and thus is quick and simple.

Today, with the high number of second marriages, it often happens that one of the remarried parties wishes to set things straight with the Church after the first spouse has died. Although the death of the first spouse dissolves the first marriage, the right to remarry under such circumstances must still be documented with a Certificate of Death. The Tribunals, especially in the United States, are seeing an increasing number of these previous bond cases.

In the United States there were about 2,000 decisions based on the previous bond ground in 1981.

III. DISSOLUTION CASES (The Catholic Divorce)

Many people do not know that the Church grants dissolutions as well as annulments. While the ease with which annulments have been granted in recent years has led some conservative voices to condemn the process as allowing a "Catholic divorce" under another name, it must be remembered that the Church quietly has been granting divorces for most of its history under the less controversial term of "dissolution." In fact, until the inception of the APN in 1970 and the later use of psychological grounds, ten times more dissolutions than annulments were granted.

The difference between a dissolution and an annulment is that a dissolution breaks a marriage bond that is acknowledged to exist; an annulment declares that the bond never existed. It is really the dissolution, then, that is most properly referred to as a "Catholic divorce." Furthermore, unlike annulment, the dissolution procedure can be traced back to early Church days. The point might be made that divorce is actually more Catholic than annulment is.

With this said, it must be added that the average American Catholic who is divorced and remarried has little hope of being granted a dissolution. The fact that at one time ten times more dissolutions than annulments were granted only reflects the tiny number of annulments that used to be granted, because at their peak dissolutions amounted to no more than 3,000 or 4,000 cases per year. Currently only about 2,000 dissolutions, as compared to more than 50,000 annulments, are granted each year in the United States. Because dissolutions are the oldest Church solutions to marital problems, and because they were once the best of bad choices for the Petitioner, some uninformed clergy may discuss only these with you, when your best approach at present is to avoid them in your petition. In point of fact, dissolutions tend to be of greatest use to new converts.

A. Two Privileges of the Faith

The Pauline Privilege   The Pauline Privilege can be used only when both parties to a valid marriage are unbaptized. If one later converts and is baptized, he or she obtains the right to break the bond and remarry if the unbelieving spouse refuses to "cohabit peacefully." That is, if the unbeliever attempts to hinder the practice of the new faith.

How It Began   In the early days of Christianity the Church was persecuted by Roman authorities and so was regularly confronted with situations in which one spouse converted and was baptized and the other refused to convert. It was not uncommon for the unbelieving spouse to be openly hostile to the new religion in ways that endangered not only the believer's faith but his or her life as well. There is no doubt that the Church frowned on divorce even under these circumstances, and St. Paul encouraged believers to remain with their unbelieving partners if they could. Still, it was possible for the situation to become intolerable, and St. Paul decided that in such circumstances the preservation of the faith took priority over even the marriage bond. He tells his people in I Corinthians 7:15:

> If the unbeliever wishes to separate, however, let him do so. The believing husband or wife is not bound in such cases. God has called you to live in peace.

Using this text as a starting point, the Church began to hammer out its position on marriage and the relationship between marriage and faith. The first teaching to appear was the Pauline Privilege, so called because of its reference to the passage from St. Paul. It is based on the assumption that a marriage between two unbaptized persons is only a "natural bond," and therefore can be broken if it is "for the good of the faith" to do so.

How It Works   An individual who wishes to take advantage of the Pauline Privilege must prove that the unbelieving spouse refuses to cohabit peacefully. As a matter of procedure, formal questions or interpellations (also sometimes called "interrogatories") must be put to the former spouse to find out if he or she is also willing to receive baptism or if he or she is at least willing to cohabit peacefully with the baptized party without insult to the Creator. Any refusal to allow the Christian to practice the new faith in peace or an insistence on certain practices (such as artificial birth control) violative of the "new life" constitutes a ground for the granting of a dissolution under the Pauline Privilege. Refusal of the nonbeliever to cooperate in answering the questions is usually taken as evidence of the intention to refuse to cohabit peacefully. Doubts in such matters are allowed to be resolved "in favor of the faith," which means for the benefit of the baptized party. It should be remembered, however, that if the newly baptized person and not the unbeliever is the cause of the lack of peaceful cohabitation, the exercise of the Pauline Privilege will not be allowed.

The processing of such cases is not particularly difficult or expensive. They may be decided at the local level by the diocesan Tribunal, as opposed to the other type of privilege case, where papal power dissolves the marriage. In Pauline Privilege cases, the "natural bond" marriage is dissolved by the new convert when he or she consummates a sacramental marriage with a baptized spouse. Under the New Code, if the local bishop grants permission, it is even possible to invoke the Pauline Privilege when the divorced convert's second marriage is to a nonbaptized person.

The biggest problem with the Pauline Privilege in the United States, with its high percentage of Christians, is that it has a highly restricted application. Since the Catholic Church recognizes almost all Christian baptisms as valid, regardless of denomination, it is a rather rare marriage in this country in which both parties are unbaptized. When you reflect that of this already restricted group (i.e., involving a prior marriage of two nonbaptized persons) the Pauline Privilege applies, as a practical matter, only where (a) one party converts to Catholicism and (b) there is a divorce, it is surprising that as many as 500 to 600 of these dissolutions are granted each year in the United States.

Example One Two Cambodian refugees who were raised as Buddhists come to the United States. One becomes a Roman Catholic and is baptized. The other ridicules the faith and refuses to allow the Catholic to attend church. This would be an obvious case for the Pauline Privilege after the civil divorce.

Example Two Two Americans who were raised as Quakers

(and therefore not baptized) marry. One later is baptized and becomes a Catholic. They have been using artificial birth control methods all their married life and the non-Catholic refuses to discontinue their use. The marriage is shaky anyway and the non-Catholic finally moves out and obtains a civil divorce. It is not likely that the Church would raise any objection to the use of the Pauline Privilege in this case.

Example Three A Jewish woman and an atheist man who has had no religious background marry and are later divorced. The woman becomes a Catholic convert and is baptized. The former husband refuses to cooperate in any way and will not answer any of the interpellations sent to him. The wife and several friends have heard him say that he was never baptized, but no proof exists. Chances are that the Pauline Privilege will be allowed in this case since the believer is given the benefit of the doubt. If serious doubt exists, this might become a Petrine Privilege case, which we will discuss next.

See Canons #1143–1150 in the *Canons of Marriage* in Appendix I of this book for further information about the Pauline Privilege.

The Petrine Privilege Like the Pauline Privilege, the Petrine Privilege is concerned with baptism. According to this privilege, a marriage in which at least one of the parties is not baptized at the time of the wedding may be dissolved "in favor of the faith." The term "Privilege of the Faith" is used almost exclusively for this privilege. That is somewhat confusing, since the Pauline Privilege is also granted "in favor of the faith." At any event, the term Petrine Privilege is used in these instances because the privilege derives its authority directly from the power of the pope as the successor of St. Peter.

How It Began As the early Church grew and spread, situations began to arise in which baptized Christians sometimes married unbaptized partners. It became necessary to decide if these marriages were sacramental. In line with the reasoning of the Pauline Privilege, the early Church decided that it required two baptized Christians to make a sacramental union and consequently, marriages between a baptized and a nonbaptized person were to be considered only "natural" bonds. It was further decided that the papacy, using its power as the pastor of Christian souls, could grant a request of dissolution if it was deemed to be for the good of the faith to do so. Msgr. Kelleher has quipped that this gives the Pope absolute authority over all marriages except Catholic ones. While this is not exactly true, it does mean that the Pope has the power to grant a petition for dissolution of all nonsacramental marriages and therefore expands considerably the group that can petition for a privilege dissolution.

How It Works Use of the Petrine Privilege requires that one of the members of the original marriage be unbaptized at the time of the union. It must be noted that this privilege cannot be invoked if at some time while they are married both partners become baptized Christians. If this should happen, the marriage automatically becomes sacramental as soon as it is consummated (i.e., as soon as the partners, who are now both Christians, have intercourse). This is true even if the baptism is into some Christian denomination other than Catholicism.

With this in mind, however, it can be said that this privilege can be applied fairly widely. For one thing, it does not require a conversion in order to operate. The Petitioner could be the previously unbaptized party who has now been baptized, but it could also be the baptized party now converted to Catholicism, or perhaps even a Catholic who married a nonbaptized partner with a dispensation for disparity of worship. (The impediment of disparity of worship is explained on page 66.) Msgr. Kelleher refers to the Privilege of the Faith as something of a "rubber bag term" that is invoked to preserve the faith of a new convert, an old Catholic, or their children, as the Church sees fit.*
As a result, this is one of the few types of *dissolution* petitions that offer any possibilities to the average divorced Catholic. Before 1970, attempts were made to stretch this privilege to fit every possible circumstance, and in fact such farfetched actions were probably one of the reasons for the adoption of the APN and the great broadening of annulment grounds and procedures.

The Petrine Privilege is not as popular as it once was. This is

---

Kelleher, Divorce and Remarriage for Catholics, p. 43.

because, with the liberalization of annulment grounds, there are easier ways for a divorced and remarried Catholic to get right with the Church. The Petrine Privilege requires interpellations similar to those used in a Pauline Privilege case, but the real drawback is the fact that the petition must be sent all the way to Rome. Unlike the Pauline Privilege cases, which can be decided at the local level, only the pope may dissolve marriages in Petrine Privilege cases. As a result, they take a long time and are more expensive in comparison to annulment cases. Still, in 1981, about 1,400 American cases resulted in the granting of dissolutions through the use of the Petrine Privilege.

Example One   A Jewish man marries a Protestant woman. They later divorce. The man becomes a baptized Catholic and wishes to marry a Catholic. The Pauline Privilege could not be invoked in this case because the former spouse was a baptized Christian. It is unlikely that any objection would be raised to dissolving the marriage "in favor of the faith" of the new convert and the Petrine Privilege undoubtedly would be granted.

Example Two   A Roman Catholic woman marries a Protestant man with a dispensation for disparity of worship. The husband's denomination does not believe in infant baptism and as a result he is not baptized at the time of the wedding. After they are separated, he is baptized as a Protestant but they do not cohabit again and soon obtain a civil divorce.

Very clear proof would be needed in this case that the couple never had intercourse again after the man's baptism. Though they were both Christians at the time of the wedding, the husband's lack of baptism made their marriage only a natural bond, but any physical union after his baptism would automatically sacramentalize the relationship. This case could go either way, depending on the proofs available.

One of the surprises of the New Code is that there is no reference to the Petrine Privilege. The canons of the proposed New Code, which had seemed to contain a broadening of the Petrine Privilege, were never adopted. Some people at first felt that the failure to include the privilege in the New Code meant that it had been repealed. But it must be remembered that the Petrine Privilege is ultimately founded upon the inherent power of the Pope as successor of St. Peter. Thus the Petrine Privilege will continue. I believe its use will diminish, however, while at the same time the various other grounds for annulment expand.

B. Nonconsummation

Officially called "ratum non-consummatum" cases, these are simply situations in which no completed sexual intercourse took place between the wedded couple. In such cases, the marriage can be dissolved even if both parties are baptized Christians.

How It Began Again, as an extension of the papal power growing out of the privilege of the faith, it was established long ago that the pope has the authority to dissolve sacramental unions that have not been consummated. The reasoning is that if a consummated union is binding only if both partners are baptized, then the reverse is also true: A union between two baptized Christians, in order to be binding, must be consummated. Consummation is by performance of the conjugal act, and the conjugal act is defined as one suitable for the generation of offspring.

How It Works However this may have worked in the Middle Ages, such cases now require a great deal of concrete evidence, often of a medical nature. Once again, the case must be sent all the way to Rome before a decision can be made.* These are among the most lengthy cases.

For various reasons, nonconsummation seems to be the only ground many Catholics have heard about, and Catholics often have the vague idea that they must prove nonconsummation to obtain an annulment. The question is often asked: "How could I possibly petition for an annulment when I've had three chil-

---

*In July of 1972 certain procedures were adopted allowing nonconsummation cases to be processed locally if done in conformity with strict guidelines. It is not known if these local procedures will be allowed under the New Code. Canon #1142 only provides for such dissolutions "by the Roman Pontiff."

dren?" In fact, as I have stated before, the presence of children in no way lessens the possibility of obtaining an annulment.

Generally speaking, the ground of nonconsummation should not be used unless clear evidence exists. The Church Courts are naturally suspicious of such a claim and will investigate it thoroughly. Though the ground of nonconsummation served a purpose in the past, there are very few dissolutions granted on these grounds nowadays. For example, of the 165 American dioceses listing statistics on annulments and dissolutions in 1981, only 7 dioceses showed any dissolutions based on nonconsummation, and 4 of these dioceses had only one or two cases. It certainly is not the best approach to take today. In almost all instances nowadays where a petitioner might be able to petition for dissolution based on nonconsummation, he or she could also obtain an annulment today based on other grounds.

Example One A Catholic couple marry but the husband proves to be impotent, and so they are unable to consummate the marriage.

This case would be better approached as a petition for annulment on the ground of impotence. Similar evidence would be necessary, but it could be decided at the local level instead of possible remittance to Rome.

Example Two A young Catholic couple marry, and the man, a member of the armed services, is immediately shipped overseas. The parties do not consummate the marriage before he leaves, and upon his return the husband institutes divorce or civil annulment proceedings.

Unless the wife has medical proof of virginity, they may have a difficult time proving nonconsummation. In today's Tribunals, this would probably be better approached as a lack of due discretion case based upon immaturity. The couple clearly married in haste and appear not to have grasped the nature of the lifelong commitment involved.

Other instances of nonconsummation are:

Example Three Outright refusal by one party to have intercourse. It makes no difference whether the refusal was due to fear, ignorance, or other reason.

Example Four   A proxy marriage that was never consummated. Whether the nonconsummation was due to unintentional nonaccess of the parties is immaterial.

IV. OTHER GROUNDS FOR ANNULMENT

As previously discussed, the majority of petitions for formal annulment presented to the diocesan Tribunals today are based on the psychological grounds of lack of due discretion or lack of due competence. Most of the rest are based on either partial simulation or force and fear. A good number of petitions go through quickly as informal documentary cases. Though the foregoing constitute an overwhelming percentage of the grounds in use today, it is well to know about some of the other options open to you.

Though they have limited application, the following grounds include the rest of the grounds for annulment. These are based primarily upon various other defects of consent and upon what the Church calls "impediments." A few are of little more than historical value, but others may be of use to some seeking an annulment. They are listed by the New Code number as set forth in Appendix I.

#1083: Lack of Age   The age of consent is 14 for a girl and 16 for a boy. Even if the state or the Conference of Bishops establishes a higher age requirement, the above ages make the marriage valid in the Church. Ignoring state laws or local church requirements of a higher age makes the marriage illicit, but does not invalidate it. It is rare in the United States today for this ground to be used. Of course, even if only one of the parties was under the age of consent an annulment could be granted.

#1084: Impotence   Because completed sexual union is necessary to consummate a sacramental marriage, impotence on the part of either party invalidates the marriage. Some well-known cases recently upheld this principle. The ground of impotence will almost always have reference to the man, but a woman is considered to be impotent if she cannot receive the semen in the vagina and allow it to proceed to the uterus. Impotence remains a strong ground for a petition for annulment. It is not necessary, by the way, that this be physical impotence. It can be due to functional (psychological) as well as an organic cause. It can also be relative as well as absolute—that is, a person can be impotent with one partner but not with others. Consequently, impotence is not quite so narrow a ground as it may first appear. As mentioned before, most Petitioners who were in a nonconsummated union should attempt to gain an annulment based on impotence rather than a dissolution based on nonconsummation.

Of course, we want to keep in mind that fact that sterility is not the same as impotence. Sterility is neither an impediment to marriage nor a ground for annulment.

#1086: Disparity of Worship The ground of disparity of worship applies to marriages between a Catholic and a nonbaptized person. It should be distinguished from an interfaith marriage in which two baptized persons, one Catholic and one non-Catholic, are married. If a Catholic and a nonbaptized person marry without a dispensation, a case for annulment can be made. Be aware that some Christian denominations do not require baptism, or require it only for adults. In the past, in order to acquire the dispensation necessary for marriage, the non-Catholic was required to promise to allow the children to be raised in the Catholic faith. A refusal to honor this promise was usually an adequate ground for an annulment. Recently these requirements regarding the raising of children as Catholics have been eased somewhat, which makes it a bit harder to prove the repudiation of the promised conditions of dispensation, which in turn makes it more difficult to successfully petition for annulment. Anyone, though, who encountered difficulty in the practice of his or her faith, or was not allowed by the spouse to raise the children as Catholics, should definitely consider a couple of possible alternative grounds for annulment. If there has been difficulty in practicing one's faith, several other grounds also might be available, including the reserved or conditional nature of the consent. The expanded fraud ground in the New Code (see Canon #1098) may also be a primary or alternate ground in such cases.

#1087 and #1088: Sacred Orders and Religious Vows Priests, deacons, subdeacons, and members of religious orders who have pronounced solemn vows may not marry without first obtaining a dispensation. In the turbulent 1960s and early 1970s, some of these people simply "dropped out" and married. Without the required dispensation, however, the marriage is invalid. It should be added that simple vows (as distinguished from solemn vows) make marriage illicit but not invalid. The distinction is an ecclesiastical one with which those involved are familiar.

#1089: Abduction A woman who is carried off and forced to marry is married invalidly. I mention this only to dispel the notion that an elopement might fall under this category. It does not. The abduction must be forced. In days of old this ground was sometimes used when a woman was abducted because her family had arranged a marriage in which she was not consulted.

#1090: Murder Another interesting curiosity on the list of impediments. If you or your current spouse murdered your former partner in order to marry each other, you are currently in an invalid union. Wouldn't it be something to see someone present this as ground for an annulment? Needless to say, it is seldom used. I've always thought that using this ground to annul a marriage would be a bit like the story of the youth who was brought before the judge to answer to a charge of murdering his parents: the youngster admitted the dastardly deed but threw himself on the mercy of the court, claiming that he was, after all, an orphan boy.

#1091: Consanguinity Blood relatives may not marry if the relationship is close. Direct descendants and brothers and sisters may never marry validly, nor may first cousins. There are impediments to marriage that require dispensation down through third cousins. Civil laws, incidentally, are usually just as much if not more restrictive.

#1092: *Affinity*   The ground of affinity extends the consanguinity impediment to the relationship between you and the family of your former spouse, that is, your former in-laws. You cannot marry your former mother-in-law, father-in-law, son-in-law, daughter-in-law, or stepchild, even if your former spouse is deceased.

#1093: *Public Propriety*   The ground of public propriety is an extension of the consanguinity and affinity impediments to cover cases of common law marriages or other informal sexual liaisons. A common law marriage is one in which the parties live together without compliance with either Church or civil form or ceremony. The intent of the public propriety ground is to make sure that there is no possibility of marriage between natural blood relatives down to the second degree in the man's direct descending line or to the blood relatives of the woman, and vice versa.

#1094: *Legal Relationship*   You are not allowed to marry someone whom you have legally adopted or who is closely related in the direct or collateral line to the adopted person.

#1096: *Ignorance*   If a party has no idea that marriage is supposed to be a permanent relationship or involves the procreation of children, the marriage is invalid. Except in the cases of children or the mentally retarded it seems unlikely that this would occur. Ignorance is not presumed after puberty. Of course in the case of children there may be the additional ground of lack of age, as discussed earlier.

#1097: *Error of Person*   Traditionally, the defect of consent based on error of person was applied only to cases of actual physical substitution or to an error concerning the *quality* of the marriage partner that was so basic that it in effect amounted to a case of mistaken identity. So, in the strictest sense, when Jacob thought he was marrying Rachel and afterward found out he had married Leah instead, he was a victim of error of person. But the ground of error of person has been broadened considerably in recent years.

Tribunals now include more and more errors considering

the quality of the partner in determining whether annulments should be granted upon this ground. After a series of cases, the Church has arrived at its present position, which allows an annulment where one of the parties can show that there has been a substantial error made regarding the quality of his or her partner. This error of quality must be (a) true, (b) present at the time of the marriage, (c) grave, (d) unknown to the Petitioner at the time of the marriage, (e) fraudulently concealed for the purpose of obtaining marital consent, and (f) the cause of a crisis upon discovery by the Petitioner.*

In the Wrona-Caracara case the Petitioner obtained an annulment based upon the fact that the Respondent had concealed from her a prior marriage. In earlier times, such concealment would never have resulted in an annulment based on error of person.

So you should be aware of the expanded possibilities for annulments under the error of quality of person ground. Many times such error has strong elements of fraud, and such fraud might in some cases serve as an alternate ground or as a ground for annulment in its own right.

#1098: Fraud   There is a very positive change in the treatment of fraud under the New Code. The ground of fraud has in effect been upgraded and now has its own separate category. Under the Old Code it was found under the heading of error of person. If deliberate deception was used to obtain consent, and if the matter concealed seriously disturbs the marriage relationship, the marriage contract is invalid. A specific case is one in which a sterile person deliberately conceals the sterility in order to obtain marital consent. If you knew about your spouse's sterility and wanted to marry anyway, the condition would not be invalidating; but if it was intentionally concealed from you in order to obtain your consent, this constitutes an invalidating fraud. Thus a young man concealing a vasectomy or a woman her tubal ligation might fit into this category.

#1101–1102: Simulated and Conditional Consent   We have already talked about the "big three" of simulated consent. Similarly, if one party has an internal reservation about abiding by

* Lawrence G. Wrenn, Decisions (Wrona-Caracara case), p. 136.

some other essential element of the marriage, the marriage is invalid. In order to obtain an annulment based upon such reservation of consent, your main obstacle will be to show that the reservation involved a serious and essential matter regarding the marriage.

Conditional consent refers to any extrinsic condition placed on the marriage that might make the union invalid. Thus the woman who marries under the condition that her spouse become a dentist or the man who marries on the condition that his wife never grow fat might be said to have only "conditionally consented" to their union. It is very difficult to prove, however, that such conditions regarding the future existed at the time of the marriage.

4

The Cost of an Annulment

I. MYTHOLOGY AND MISINFORMATION

Few subjects are touchier than the question of annulment costs. Many people seeking annulments feel angry that, in addition to having to go through a trying process, they are expected also to pay for it. Church officials seem embarrassed that there is any charge and are very reluctant to discuss real dollars and cents figures, which leads inquirers to expect the worst. Because of the sensitivity and defensiveness about costs, a great mythology has built up. A casual survey I conducted among Catholic laity of my own acquaintance turned up the following misconceptions:

Annulments are very expensive. (I heard estimates of $3,000 to $25,000.)

The Church is primarily interested in the money. (If you are rich, annulments are easy.)

The Church is making a bundle off all these annulments. (After all, what does it cost them?)

Whatever the official fees, a lot has to be passed under the table.

I do not know why people are willing to believe the worst about their own Church on this matter, but even the limited information available to the public on this subject should lay such rumors to rest. The fee charged for annulments, far from enriching the Church, does not even cover the cost of the processing. Every effort is made to keep charges to a minimum. The first thing told to anyone inquiring about fees is that whether a Petitioner is able to pay will have no bearing on the ruling on the petition. On a typical general information sheet for Petitioners, as seen in Form A of Appendix II, the following statement is underlined:

> However, under no circumstances is the progress of a case contingent on the Petitioner's financial ability or willingness to pay.

Note that it says "willingness" as well as "financial ability to pay." That means that you can outright refuse to pay and the case would still go through, a far cry from the incredible misconceptions that prevail. Clearly the Church has no intention of making the fee an obstacle on the road to annulment nor a means of acquiring wealth.

II. METHODS OF CHARGING

Just how the Tribunal charges are determined varies from diocese to diocese. Charges also vary from case to case, depending on the expenses incurred in the investigation. Some dioceses use a sliding scale of charges that depend on the Petitioner's income. Others average the secretarial costs, dividing them by the number of cases processed; thus the charges would go down as the number of cases go up. In others, the fee is treated more as a gratuity that Tribunal officials realize will not fully cover the expense of the proceedings.

III. METHODS OF PAYMENT

Methods of payment are also flexible. As stated earlier, no diocese requires that you pay before your case can be judged. Most have some suggested installment rate, but are open to almost any rate of payment over any length of time. There are no interest rates or penalty fees. Many dioceses are willing to listen to some creative alternative plans or alternate service instead of cash payments. In at least one parish I know of, the fee is paid out of parish funds, and the parishioner is allowed to pay it back if and when he or she so desires. The rationale is that it is more pleasant to pay back your own parish than the distant Tribunal.

IV. SOME ACTUAL AMOUNTS

There is usually an initial fee of about $25 that accompanies the petition when it is submitted. From there the charges vary considerably depending on the case. People are reluctant to be pinned down about the figures, but here are some actual figures I have been able to find:

• I was told unofficially by a priest who had acted as an Advocate in the Madison, Wisconsin, Diocese that the average cost of an annulment case there was about $190.

• In *Marriage Today* Siegel says:

> The total average expenses incurred by the tribunal in each trial case are approximately $1,000. The tribunal would expect an offering not of $1,000 but $200 for the ordinary case. Of this amount $200 covers only the minimal expenses.[*]

• In *Divorce and Remarriage for Catholics*, Msgr. Kelleher says:

> In the Archdiocese of New York the expenses ranged from $25 to a maximum of $225, depending on the nature of the case. Whether a person could pay the expenses or not made no difference in our accepting a case and bringing it to a conclusion as soon as we were able.[**]

• In her book about her own annulment, *Credo*, Kay Goodnow sets out a complete fee list for the Archdiocese of Kansas City in 1976. It lists the following fees:
  (1) A regular fee of $20 at the submission of the petition

[*]*Siegel*, Marriage Today, pp. A69–A70.
[**]*Kelleher*, Divorce and Remarriage for Catholics? p. 123.

(2) A sliding scale of fees once cases are accepted:
Annual income below $10,000—$100
Annual income between $10,000-$15,000—$250
Annual income between $15,000-$20,000—$400

(3) In documentary cases and privilege cases the fees are as follows:

(a) $100 for Pauline Privilege cases
(b) $50 for documentary cases
(c) Regular fee of $80 for the local Tribunal and $120 for the Roman tax on Petrine Privilege cases
(d) Regular fee of $80 for the local Tribunal and $350 for the Roman tax on ratum non-consummatum cases

• Information provided by the Archdiocese of Chicago states that a fee of $250 is requested when the petition is accepted for decision. It can be paid either in a lump sum or in installments. If the Petitioner cannot afford the fee it is waived partially or entirely.

• The filing fee in the Lafayette, Louisiana, Diocese is a suggested amount of $250, with the alternative of a monthly billing at a suggested amount of $250.

• I know of several instances where no fee at all, not even a filing fee, was required because of the poor financial condition of the Petitioner.

Petitioners I interviewed from several dioceses consistently said that the annulment fee was either nonexistent or merely incidental to the procedure. In a couple of discussions, the Petitioners mentioned that they would have filed earlier but had been frightened away by stories of huge fees, which would have been impossible for them to pay. Contrary to what you may have heard, then, the annulment fee should be no obstacle to filing for an annulment.

5

The New Code of Canon Law

The American Procedural Norms (APN) marked the observable beginning of the change in attitude that has swept through the Church Tribunals since 1970. Pressure for the guidelines had been building for years. The Norms were first instituted for a trial period in July 1969. They were later renewed indefinitely and remained in effect until the New Code of Canon Law was promulgated. There were 23 Norms in the APN, all of which dealt with the procedure at the Tribunal, that is, they were concerned with the jurisidictional, administrative, and processing aspects of annulments.

The Norms speeded and simplified the processing of annulments in America but, when combined with the new psychological grounds, they made the United States by far the most progressive annulment jurisdiction in the world. Canadian and Australian Tribunals were given certain privileges in 1974 that paralleled some of the progressive provisions of the APN.

I. EFFICIENCY WAS ENCOURAGED

Many of the Norms suggested time limits for various stages along the way toward a ruling. For example, Norm #6 set a guideline of six months for the whole process, from the formal acceptance of the petition to the final decision. These were ideals, of course, and often were not met. But they represented an important change in attitude. They clearly indicated that the Tribunals were not to let cases languish or drag on forever.

This encouragement of quick, efficient handling of cases obviously meant that more petitions could be handled.

We have already discussed the fact that the APN granted much more latitude than previously in allowing forum shopping; in allowing decisions by one instead of three judges; and in, for all practical purposes, doing away with the old automatic appeal required by the 1917 Code.

II. AND NOW THE NEW CODE

Mostly as a result of its own success, the APN came under fire from some who wanted to see the number of annulments drastically reduced. For this reason, the marriage canons of the New Code of Canon Law, which had been in preparation since Pope John XXIII began the process some years ago, became the focus of controversy. Since the New Code was to supersede the APN, there naturally was much anxiety about what changes it would bring to the existing liberal approach to annulments in the United States. With Pope John Paul II expressing concern over the rapid growth of annulments, many pessimists feared a return to the past.

What has happened, though, is that although certain procedural changes have been regressive, the *substantive* changes are very progressive. As mentioned in Chapter 3, the all-important psychological grounds have been spelled out explicitly in the New Code, and there has been a broadening of grounds such as force and fear and fraud.

III. THE EFFECT OF THE NEW CODE

One thing that can be said with certainty is that no change in canon law will bring back the old days in the Marriage Tribunals. While the American Procedural Norms and the Canadian and Australian procedures have been superseded, the general spirit fostered by them will continue. If restrictive interpretations are attempted to be forced on the Tribunals, it will only lead, Fr. Andrew Greeley has remarked, to more Internal Forum annulments and an avoidance of the institutional procedures. (Chapter 6 talks about the Internal Forum approach.) As Greeley said:

> [I]n fact, annulments will continue, only now they will be granted in the rectory parlor by parish priests or in the bedrooms by Catholic lay people.... Those laity who decide for themselves that their first marriage was invalid will, if they still care about the rules of the institutional Church, consult with a sympathetic priest. The others will simply make their own decision.*

But most divorced people will not have to resort to such alternatives if they give Tribunals a chance. The reinstitution of an automatic review may well add some time to the process, and it may initially cut down on the number of annulments granted annually because of the extended waiting period, but it is not likely to lead to more negative rulings. The Tribunals in America have changed drastically in the past dozen years. They are now largely staffed by people who see their role as helping, rather than hindering, the person seeking an annulment. This will not change even though the Norms have been superseded.

Although some fear that the review courts may be loaded with "obstructionists," it is my feeling that for both practical and canonical reasons, the mandatory review will not make any difference in the number of annulments granted.

On the practical side, suffice it to say that such a court-stacking maneuver would simply not be realistic today. And canonically, any decision of the Tribunal, which has been reached with moral certainty and on proper grounds (including psychological grounds), cannot be easily disregarded.

Remember that the priests serving at all levels of the process are men of good will who have seen many recent changes in the Church, are the "survivors" of the turmoil of the 1960s and 1970s, and are being presented with a growing avalanche of annulment petitions. They will not allow themselves to be used. I believe that the review judges will call them as they see them, and that they will see them just as their Court of First Instance brethren do. And after all, those serving on review

*Greeley, The Witness (Dubuque), March 26, 1981.

panels are often the very same people serving as judges in Courts of First Instance in other jurisdictions. Inconsistent rulings are simply not in the books.

It is my belief that the Church does not want to make itself irrelevant on the divorce and remarriage issue as it did on the birth control question.

One important concept of the New Code is the emphasis on the "principle of subsidiarity." In other words, much greater authority is now vested in the various national episcopal conferences. In the United States, Canada, and Australia, for example, it is generally conceded that the bishops will do all they can to try to continue the reconciliation being achieved by flexible, realistic annulment procedures.

6

The Internal Forum
and Other Approaches

Let us suppose you have gone through the Tribunal process and have been denied an annulment. It does happen. I have emphasized repeatedly how likely you are to succeed, but even a Tribunal with 90 percent acceptance of petitions necessarily rejects 10 percent of the petitions. If you are unfortunate enough to fall into the minority whose petition is ruled on unfavorably, you are still not forever barred from full communion. It is time to look into the Internal Forum.

In addition to the Tribunal process that we have been discussing, there is a second method of returning to the good graces of the Church that you may wish to consider. The Internal Forum, or so-called "Good Conscience" solution, is a method whereby a person who has been divorced and remarried can, with the aid of a sympathetic priest, quietly return to full communion without being granted an annulment.

The important distinction here is between the External Forum, made up of the Tribunal system, and the Internal Forum, which refers to the individual's relationship with God. The Tribunals are, of necessity, concerned with circumstances that can be objectively proven. Because of the general presumption of the validity of marriages, Tribunal judges cannot speculate wildly outside the record in an annulment proceeding. But even the Church is aware that a Tribunal decision and the truth may not always coincide. Fr. Young says, "Canonical conformity and righteousness before the Lord are not identical. Frequently the truth as known to God is not the truth as perceived by the community. . . . The conscientious decisions of couples should be respected even if contrary to Church order."* In other words, if you know (i.e., internally) that your marriage was invalid but for some reason cannot prove it in a Tribunal case, you may still be able to return to full communion with good conscience.

This could happen in any number of situations. For example, perhaps your spouse confessed privately to you an intention to never have children or remain faithful, but refuses to admit this to the Tribunal. Or perhaps witnesses who could have proved your case have died, cannot be located, or refuse to testify. Maybe documents or other evidence necessary for your case are for some reason unobtainable. You then have no way of proving what you know to be a fact—that your marriage was invalid. The Tribunal, as a court of law, must be presented with sufficient evidence to prove annulment grounds. If the evidence is not presented, a favorable ruling is not possible. The External Forum cannot help you in your rightful attempt to be free of this invalid marriage.

Then again, perhaps the luck of the draw placed your petition within the jurisdiction of a Tribunal that is practically nonfunctioning or that simply does not grant annulments as readily as others.

This is where the Internal Forum becomes useful. It is not an official process, though there are certain guidelines. An important element of the Internal Forum is the quiet consultation with a priest, often beginning in the privacy of the confessional. The priest, acting as the judge in the Tribunal of Mercy** will do what he deems necessary to help you, a penitent, form a good conscience and return to full communion. The Church has always accepted the possibility of this solution though it obviously wishes you to approach the External Forum first.

Even before the time of Luther, the Church has been leery of resorting to individual *subjective* norms of morality. The fear has been that there might be no "norms" at all. Everyone could do his or her own thing. But morality ultimately reflects your own individual decision made after seeking out a rightly formed conscience. Involving a priest is your attempt to form a

*Young, Ministering to the Divorced Catholic, p. 146.
**Catoir, Catholics and Broken Marriage, p. 55.

right conscience when resorting to the Internal Forum. And, after all is said and done, the External Forum must take a back seat to the Church maxim "Suprema lex salus animarum," or, "The Supreme law is the saving of souls." And the Internal Forum may be the last best chance for some people to do just that.

QUESTIONS

Didn't I Read a While Back That Rome Had Rejected This Whole Idea?

No. The Internal Forum has not been ruled illegal by Rome. What happened was that a good deal of publicity erupted a few years ago when bishops in some dioceses set up a standardized, semiofficial procedure for the Internal Forum solution. The problem was that this amounted to a new External Forum procedure. An externalized Internal Forum is, of course, a contradiction in terms. From the Vatican's viewpoint it appeared to be a way of circumventing the official machinery that the Church had set up for reconciliation.

It appeared that an option was developing to the Tribunal annulment.

While many believe that this method may ultimately be the new method for reconciling divorced and remarried Catholics with the Church, unless or until it is officially accepted, it must remain a private and unofficial one. The bishops, realizing this, acknowledged the possible dangers of this "option," and withdrew their backing for such a solution. But it should be noted that Rome did not reject the private use of the Internal Forum; it only rejected the public institution of it as an alternative to the Tribunal hearing. "Rome didn't want a new public law or custom developing which would put aside the procedural laws of the Code. This has nothing to do with what happens in the confessional or the private thoughts of the individual."*

So It Is Only the Official Adoption of the Internal Forum That Has Been Banned, Not the Private Use?

Exactly.

* *Ibid.*, p. 57.

But Haven't Some Bishops Refused to Allow Its Use in Their Diocese?

Some bishops have definitely discouraged the Internal Forum. Many priests are reluctant to get involved in the process because of the general confusion just discussed. But its use is not immoral, and a careful search will turn up a priest not too far away who will privately undertake to assist you in applying the Good Conscience solution to your own case.

How Can He Do That?

You must remember the importance of conscience in the attribution of sin. The Document on Religious Freedom of Vatican II reemphasizes this. Sin has to do with a person's relationship with God, and not, ultimately, with his or her relationship with the institutional Church. If a person knows internally but cannot prove externally that his or her first marriage was invalid, he or she is justified in God's eyes in returning to the sacraments. The Church, therefore, under those circumstances, must accept the person's decision of conscience and allow him or her to return.

How Do I Go About Invoking the Internal Forum Solution?

First, do not think of it as an easy alternative to the annulment process. Almost all priests will advise you to try the official route first. Second, be sure you honestly feel your first marriage was not valid. One of the clearest indications of this is your own feeling of sin. If you feel no sense of sin in your present state, you may well be justified in believing your first marriage was not a truly sacramental union. Of course you must be objective and arrive at a rightly formed conscience. Finally, through a Catholic divorce support group or someone else who has used the Internal Forum solution, obtain the name of a priest you may approach on the subject. Talk it over with him privately.

What Is Involved in the Process?

The priest will discuss the situation with you thoroughly.

He will probably ask you to briefly study the Catholic teaching on marriage again. He will be looking for your evidence of stability in your present marriage and willingness to assume responsibilities incurred in both marriages, your awareness of your own culpability and real repentance for your share of the blame in the broken marriage, and finally, and most importantly, your state of conscience. Do you honestly believe you are not in a state of unrepentant sin? If all these things add up favorably, he will give you absolution and readmit you to the sacraments. Note that privacy is of the essence here. The Internal Forum can only be used if it is done without scandal. Don't advertise the situation; just quietly make use of it to regain full access to the Church.

But What If I Believe My First Marriage Was Valid?

Find a priest who uses the Internal Forum and discuss it. You may be wrong. You must ask yourself if you feel your first marriage was valid *by Church standards*. That is all that matters in this case, not a secular or personal feeling. If you truly believe your second marriage is wrong, you may well see it as an adulterous union and honestly believe that you are still married to your first spouse. Is that what you think? Chances are you simply believe your first marriage was a real one by all secular and personal standards, but that it died and you are now in a second, equally valid, marriage. That position, however, is one that is currently impossible to take in dealing with Church law. The Church law can only see you as bound for life to your first spouse, or never bound at all (except in the rare cases of dissolution discussed in Chapter 3). Which of these two best describes your own condition? What is at issue here is how you feel your first marriage would be interpreted by the Church's very strict definition of validity. So far as your relationship with the Church is concerned, other standards are irrelevant.

Castelli notes in *What the Church Is Doing for Divorced and Remarried Catholics* that the Canon Law Society of America has set up a list of criteria for admitting divorced and remarried Catholics to the sacraments. The following is a paraphrase of these criteria:

(1) Is the first marriage dead and reconciliation impossible? (Here an uncontested divorce or the remarriage of either party is likely to be sufficient evidence.)
(2) Are the financial obligations, such as child support and alimony, being met?
(3) Does the second marriage show signs of permanence? (Length, stability, and children are all indications.)
(4) Is there a willingness to lead the Christian life in an ecclesiastical community? (The desire to return to the sacraments is a good sign of this.)

Also, according to Castelli, some priests are willing to use the Internal Forum to readmit people who insist that their first marriage was valid but they now consider it dead.

In approaching the Internal Forum, ask yourself: Have I gone through the Tribunal process? If not, why not? If I have gone to the Tribunal and my petition has been rejected, was it on mere jurisdictional grounds? Do I feel it was because I had no grounds for annulment, or was it because I have grounds but could not muster enough objective proof to overcome the legal presumption of validity? If your failure was one of insufficient proof of a fact you know to be true, you may well be able to resort to the Internal Forum.

Although the Internal Forum may give relief to some Catholics, I do not think that the Internal Forum provides the final answer for this issue. I think the Church is presently caught up in one of the great transitions it periodically faces. A more permanent relief may well evolve from the lack of due competence annulment ground which, as discussed in Chapter 3, recognizes that marriage is an ongoing *covenant*. This ground embraces the concept that if a person is not psychologically competent to carry out the marriage contract (even if all the elements of consent appeared to be present at the time of the ceremony), a civilly dead marriage can be annulled.

A civil attorney would approach the contractual question somewhat differently, but probably end up with the same result. For example, it seems to me that it would be helpful for the Church to incorporate the legal concept of the requirement of mutual performance by delivery of "consideration" in a continuing contract. In other words, it should be acknowledged that the marriage contract is not legally "performed" at the altar, but rather only as each party gives love and loyalty to the other on a daily basis over the years.

Arguably, the marriage contract is a contract so long as both parties perform upon those vows as the marriage goes on. When one party refuses or fails to perform (that is, to give the promised consideration of love necessary for the maintenance of a community of conjugal life) (see, for example, Canons #1055, #1057, #1134, and #1135 in Appendix I) it is beyond reason to insist that the "mutual" promises should be enforced against the other party. In civil law parlance, the contract has failed for want of consideration.

In no other contract is there a requirement that one party be bound to an original promise when the other contracting party refuses performance. Is the parish pastor who subscribes to a local newspaper bound to continue paying for the newspaper every week even if the paper carrier stops delivery? Must you continue to work for an employer to whom you have promised your services even if the employer stops paying you? Must a priest continue his duties and abide by his solemn vows of Holy Orders even if he has lost his vocation and wants to change his way of life? It would, of course, be illogical to answer yes to any of these questions.

Thus it is perhaps just as illogical to require that a party be bound to continue abiding by the terms of the marriage contract—that is, to continue delivering marital consideration—when the parties are civilly divorced, living apart and in many cases, living with other spouses.

A possible advantage to using this "failure of consideration" approach vis-à-vis the lack of due competence ground is that failure of consideration does not require proof of insanity or even psychological incompetence to give consent. In any event, the "lack of consideration" approach might well be examined in more detail by canon lawyers, and it seems to go hand-in-hand with the lack of due competency ground for annulment.

Another possible approach to solving the Catholic divorce and remarriage dilemma is offered by those who suggest that only the first marriage be considered a *sacramental* marriage.

The second marriage could be recognized by the Church as a nonsacramental bond that does not result in adultery. Sister Mary Ann Walsh has proposed that

> the Catholic Church recognize second marriages in Church without calling them sacramental marriages. The Church, while maintaining that there is but one sacramental marriage and that annulments are still possible within the Church, would also acknowledge that not everyone reaches the ideal sacramental marriage.*

Sister Walsh points out that such an approach would apply to people who believe that their first marriage was sacramental and should not be erased, but who are divorced and long to remarry within the Church.

Although as I mentioned at the beginning of this book, it is not my intention to become involved in a theological critique of Catholic marriage, I will at least point out the position of those Catholics who are divorced and remarried. We are all aware of the biblical injunction that "what God has joined together, let no man separate" (Matt. 19:6). The divorced and remarried Catholic cries out in asking why the Church insists on a literal interpretation of this passage when the Church fully recognizes that dozens of other passages cannot be taken literally. I would also note that even the present Church position fails to literally interpret the biblical passage in question. For example, the Church now takes the position that the "separating" or "sundering" does not happen when the parties leave each other, move to different homes, are civilly divorced, have all their possessions divided, and have the children separated from one parent. No sin necessarily takes place when all these things happen. On the contrary, the Church holds that the separation of the marriage occurs when one of the unfortunate parties remarries and tries to live out his or her life in a second, often more stable, marriage. Let's be fair about it: The literal separation takes place when the spouses break up, divorce, and go their own way.

And even if you believe in a literal interpretation of the biblical prohibition, the point can still be made: Who truly knows

*Walsh, U.S. Catholic, September 1981.

what God has joined together? In other words, the Church acknowledges that some marriages are valid and some are not. As we have elsewhere discussed, the irretrievably broken marriages ending in civil divorce may well not, for example, have been sacramental unions joined by God. Why not have divorced Catholics simply apply for annulments and have them granted conditionally? When a priest gives absolution in the confessional, it is conditional upon the penitent having the proper contrition, intention against future sin, and performance of his or her penance. In the end, it is not possible for the priest to be sure if the sacrament of penance truly took place, just as it is not possible for the judges on the Tribunal to be sure about the validity of the marriage. Canonically, a Catholic's second marriage could then be presumed a valid marriage rather than adultery.

Whatever the future for divorced and remarried Catholics, you can be certain that the Church's final position will not be hammered out until some time after you and I are gone. So for the present, a very workable solution lies in the grounds for annulment explained in Chapter 3 of this book. If the Tribunals cannot help you, the Internal Forum (or Good Conscience) solution, as discussed earlier in this chapter, should be fully explored.

> The vast field of Indecision
> is littered with the broken bodies
> of a thousand regiments of those who,
> in sight of Rescue, paused
> to think awhile, and, while
> pausing, were trampled by the measured
> tread of Time.

I

Canons on Marriage, New Code of Canon Law*

#1055 §1. The marriage covenant, by which a man and a woman establish between themselves a partnership of their whole life, and which of its own very nature is ordered to the well-being of the spouses and to the procreation and upbringing of children, has, between the baptized, been raised by Christ the Lord to the dignity of a sacrament.

§2. Consequently, a valid marriage contract cannot exist between baptized persons without its being by that very fact a sacrament.

#1056   The essential properties of marriage are unity and indissolubility; in Christian marriage they acquire a distinctive firmness by reason of the sacrament.

#1057   §1. A marriage is brought into being by the lawfully manifested consent of persons who are legally capable. This consent cannot be supplied by any human power.

§2. Matrimonial consent is an act of will by which a man and a woman by an irrevocable covenant mutually give and accept one another for the purpose of establishing a marriage.

#1058   All can contract marriage who are not prohibited by law.

#1059   The marriage of Catholics, even if only one party is baptized, is governed not only by divine law but also by canon law, without prejudice to the competence of the civil authority in respect of the merely civil effects of the marriage.

#1060   Marriage enjoys the favor of law. Consequently, in doubt the validity of a marriage must be upheld until the contrary is proven.

#1061   §1. A valid marriage between baptized persons is said to be merely ratified, if it is not consummated; ratified and consummated,

*These canons are reprinted from The Code of Canon Law in English Translation. London: Collins, 1983; and Grand Rapids, MI: Eerdmans, 1983. Original Latin text copyright © 1983 by Libreria Editrice Vaticana, Vatican City. English translation copyright © 1983 The Canon Law Society Trust. Reprinted by permission.

if the spouses have in a human manner engaged together in a conjugal act in itself apt for the generation of offspring. To this act marriage is by its nature ordered and by it the spouses become one flesh.

§2. If the spouses have lived together after the celebration of their marriage, consummation is presumed until the contrary is proven.

§3. An invalid marriage is said to be putative if it has been celebrated in good faith by at least one party. It ceases to be such when both parties become certain of its nullity.

#1062 §1. A promise of marriage, whether unilateral or bilateral, called an engagement, is governed by the particular law which the Conference of Bishops has enacted, after consideration of such customs and civil laws as may exist.

§2. No right of action to request the celebration of marriage arises from a promise of marriage, but there does arise an action for such reparation of damages as may be due.

Chapter I: Pastoral Care and the Prerequisites for the Celebration of Marriage.

#1063 Pastors of souls are obliged to ensure that their own church community provides for Christ's faithful the assistance by which the married state is preserved in its Christian character and develops in perfection. This assistance is to be given principally:

1) by preaching, by catechetical instruction adapted to children, young people and adults, indeed by the use of the means of social communication, so that Christ's faithful are instructed in the meaning of Christian marriage and in the role of Christian spouses and parents;
2) by personal preparation for entering marriage, so that the spouses are disposed to the holiness and the obligations of their new state;
3) by the fruitful celebration of the marriage liturgy, so that it clearly emerges that the spouses manifest, and participate in, the mystery of the unity and fruitful love between Christ and the Church;
4) by the help given to those who have entered marriage, so that by faithfully observing and protecting their conjugal covenant, they may day by day achieve a holier and fuller family life.

#1064 It is the responsibility of the local Ordinary to ensure that this assistance is duly organized. If it is considered opportune, he should consult with men and women of proven experience and expertise.

#1065 §1. Catholics who have not yet received the sacrament of confirmation are to receive it before being admitted to marriage, if this can be done without grave inconvenience.

§2. So that the sacrament of marriage may be fruitfully received, spouses are earnestly recommended that they approach the sacraments of penance and the Eucharist.

#1066 Before a marriage takes place, it must be established that nothing stands in the way of its valid and lawful celebration.

#1067   The Conference of Bishops is to lay down norms concerning the questions to be asked of the parties, the publication of marriage banns, and the other appropriate means of inquiry to be carried out before marriage. Only when he has carefully observed these norms may the parish priest assist at a marriage.

#1068   In danger of death, if other proofs are not available, it suffices, unless there are contrary indications, to have the assertion of the parties, sworn if need be, that they are baptized and free of any impediment.

#1069   Before the celebration of a marriage, all the faithful are bound to reveal to the parish priest or the local Ordinary such impediments as they may know about.

#1070   If someone other than the parish priest whose function it is to assist at the marriage has made the investigations, he is by an authentic document to inform that parish priest of the outcome of these inquiries as soon as possible.

#1071   §1. Except in case of necessity, no one is to assist without the permission of the local Ordinary at:

1) the marriage of vagrants;
2) a marriage which cannot be recognized by the civil law or celebrated in accordance with it;
3) a marriage of a person for whom a previous union has created natural obligations towards a third party or towards children;
4) a marriage of a person who has notoriously rejected the Catholic faith;
5) a marriage of a person who is under censure;
6) a marriage of a minor whose parents are either unaware of it or are reasonably opposed to it;
7) a marriage to be entered by proxy, as mentioned in can. 1105.

§2. The local Ordinary is not to give permission to assist at the marriage of a person who has notoriously rejected the Catholic faith unless, with the appropriate adjustments, the norms of can. 1125 have been observed.

#1072   Pastors of souls are to see to it that they dissuade young people from entering marriage before the age customarily accepted in the region.

Chapter II: Diriment Impediments in General

#1073   A diriment impediment renders a person incapable of validly contracting a marriage.

#1074   An impediment is said to be public, when it can be proved in the external forum; otherwise, it is occult.

#1075   §1. Only the supreme authority in the Church can authentically declare when the divine law prohibits or invalidates a marriage.

§2. Only that same supreme authority has the right to establish other impediments for those who are baptized.

#1076　A custom which introduces a new impediment, or is contrary to existing impediments, is to be reprobated.

#1077　§1. The local Ordinary can in a specific case forbid a marriage of his own subjects, wherever they are residing, or of any person actually present in his territory; he can do this only for a time, for a grave reason and while that reason persists.

§2. Only the supreme authority in the Church can attach an invalidating clause to a prohibition.

#1078　§1. The local Ordinary can dispense his own subjects wherever they are residing, and all who are actually present in his territory, from all impediments of ecclesiastical law, except for those whose dispensation is reserved to the Apostolic See.

§2. The impediments whose dispensation is reserved to the Apostolic See are:

1) the impediment arising from sacred orders or from a public perpetual vow of chastity in a religious institute of pontifical right;

2) the impediment of crime mentioned in can. 1090.

§3. A dispensation is never given from the impediment of consanguinity in the direct line or in the second degree of the collateral line.

#1079　§1. When danger of death threatens, the local Ordinary can dispense his own subjects, wherever they are residing, and all who are actually present in his territory, both from the form to be observed in the celebration of marriage, and from each and every impediment of ecclesiastical law, whether public or occult, with the exception of the impediment arising from the sacred order of priesthood.

§2. In the same circumstances mentioned in §1, but only for cases in which not even the local Ordinary can be approached, the same faculty of dispensation is possessed by the parish priest, by a properly delegated sacred minister, and by the priest or deacon who assists at the marriage in accordance with can. 1116 §2.

§3. In danger of death, the confessor has the power to dispense from occult impediments for the internal forum, whether within the act of sacramental confession or outside it.

§4. In the case mentioned in §2, the local Ordinary is considered unable to be approached if he can be reached only by telegram or by telephone.

#1080　§1. Whenever an impediment is discovered after everything has already been prepared for a wedding and the marriage cannot without probable danger of grave harm be postponed until a dispensation is obtained from the competent authority, the power to dispense from all impediments, except those mentioned in can. 1078 §2(1), is possessed by the local Ordinary and, provided the case is occult, by all those mentioned in can. 1079 §§2–3, the conditions prescribed therein having been observed.

§2. This power applies also to the validation of a marriage when there is the same danger in delay and there is no time to have recourse to the Apostolic See or, in the case of impediments from which he can dispense, to the local Ordinary.

#1081   The parish priest or the priest or deacon mentioned in can. 1079 §2 should inform the local Ordinary immediately of a dispensation granted for the external forum, and this dispensation is to be recorded in the marriage register.

#1082   Unless a rescript of the Penitentiary provides otherwise, a dispensation from an occult impediment granted in the internal non-sacramental forum, is to be recorded in the book to be kept in the secret archive of the Curia. No other dispensation for the external forum is necessary if at a later stage the occult impediment becomes public.

Chapter III: Individual Diriment Impediments

#1083   §1. A man cannot validly enter marriage before the completion of his sixteenth year of age, nor a woman before the completion of her fourteenth year.

§2. The Conference of Bishops may establish a higher age for the lawful celebration of marriage.

#1084   §1. Antecedent and perpetual impotence to have sexual intercourse, whether on the part of the man or on that of the woman, whether absolute or relative, by its very nature invalidates marriage.

§2. If the impediment of impotence is doubtful, whether the doubt be one of law or one of fact, the marriage is not to be prevented nor, while the doubt persists, is it to be declared null.

§3. Without prejudice to the provisions of can. 1098, sterility neither forbids nor invalidates a marriage.

#1085   §1. A person bound by the bond of a previous marriage, even if not consummated, invalidly attempts marriage.

§2. Even though the previous marriage is invalid or for any reason dissolved, it is not thereby lawful to contract another marriage before the nullity or the dissolution of the previous one has been established lawfully and with certainty.

#1086   §1. A marriage is invalid when one of the two persons was baptized in the Catholic Church or received into it and has not by a formal act defected from it, and the other was not baptized.

§2. This impediment is not to be dispensed unless the conditions mentioned in can. 1125 and 1126 have been fulfilled.

§3. If at the time the marriage was contracted one party was commonly understood to be baptized, or if his or her baptism was doubtful, the validity of the marriage is to be presumed in accordance with can. 1060, until it is established with certainty that one party was baptized and the other was not.

#1087   §1. Those who are in sacred orders invalidly attempt marriage.

#1088   Those who are bound by a public perpetual vow of chastity in a religious institute invalidly attempt marriage.

#1089   No marriage can exist between a man and a woman who has been abducted, or at least detained, with a view to contracting a marriage with her, unless the woman, after she has been separated from her abductor and established in a safe and free place, chooses marriage of her own accord.

#1090 §1. One who, with a view to entering marriage with a particular person, has killed that person's spouse, or his or her own spouse, invalidly attempts this marriage.

§2. They also invalidly attempt marriage with each other who, by mutual physical or moral action, brought about the death of either's spouse.

#1091 §1. Marriage is invalid between those related by consanguinity in all degrees of the direct line, whether ascending or descending, legitimate or natural.

§2. In the collateral line, it is invalid up to the fourth degree inclusive.

§3. The impediment of consanguinity is not multiplied.

§4. A marriage is never to be permitted if a doubt exists as to whether the parties are related by consanguinity in any degree of the direct line, or in the second degree of the collateral line.

#1092 Affinity in any degree of the direct line invalidates marriage.

#1093 The impediment of public propriety arises when a couple live together after an invalid marriage, or from a notorious or public concubinage. It invalidates marriage in the first degree of the direct line between the man and those related by consanguinity to the woman, and vice versa.

#1094 Those who are legally related by reason of adoption cannot validly marry each other if their relationship is in the direct line or in the second degree of the collateral line.

Chapter IV: Matrimonial Consent

#1095 The following are incapable of contracting marriage:
1) those who lack sufficient use of reason;
2) those who suffer from a grave lack of discretionary judgment concerning the essential matrimonial rights and obligations to be mutually given and accepted;
3) those who, because of causes of a psychological nature, are unable to assume the essential obligations of a marriage.

#1096 §1. For matrimonial consent to exist, it is necessary that the contracting parties be at least not ignorant of the fact that marriage is a permanent partnership between a man and a woman, ordered to the procreation of children through some form of sexual cooperation.

§2. This ignorance is not presumed after puberty.

#1097 §1. Error about a person renders a marriage invalid.

§2. Error about a quality of a person, even though it be the reason for the contract, does not render a marriage invalid unless this quality is directly and principally intended.

#1098 A person contracts invalidly who enters marriage inveigled by deceit, perpetrated in order to secure consent, concerning some quality of the other party, which of its very nature can seriously disrupt the partnership of conjugal life.

#1099 Provided it does not determine the will, error concerning the unity or the indissolubility or the sacramental dignity of marriage does not vitiate matrimonial consent.

#1100 Knowledge of or opinion about the nullity of a marriage does not necessarily exclude matrimonial consent.

#1101 §1. The internal consent of the mind is presumed to conform to the words or the signs used in the celebration of a marriage.

§2. If, however, either or both of the parties should by a positive act of will exclude marriage itself or any essential element of marriage or any essential property, such party contracts invalidly.

#1102 §1. Marriage cannot be validly contracted subject to a condition concerning the future.

§2. Marriage entered into subject to a condition concerning the past or the present is valid or not, according as whatever is the basis of the condition exists or not.

§3. However, a condition as mentioned in §2 may not lawfully be attached except with the written permission of the local Ordinary.

#1103 A marriage is invalid which was entered into by reason of force or of grave fear imposed from outside, even if not purposely, from which the person has no escape other than by choosing marriage.

#1104 §1. To contract marriage validly it is necessary that the contracting parties be present together, either personally or by proxy.

§2. The spouses are to express their matrimonial consent in words; if, however, they cannot speak, then by equivalent signs.

#1105 §1. For a marriage by proxy to be valid, it is required:

1) that there be a special mandate to contract with a specific person;
2) that the proxy be designated by the mandator and personally discharge this function;

§2. For the mandate to be valid, it is to be signed by the mandator, and also by the parish priest or local Ordinary of the place in which the mandate is given or by a priest delegated by either of them or by at least two witnesses, or it is to be drawn up in a document which is authentic according to the civil law.

§3. If the mandator cannot write, this is to be recorded in the mandate and another witness added who is also to sign the document; otherwise, the mandate is invalid.

§4. If the mandator revokes the mandate, or becomes insane, before the proxy contracts in his or her name, the marriage is invalid, even though the proxy or the other contracting party is unaware of the fact.

#1106 Marriage can be contracted through an interpreter, but the parish priest may not assist at such a marriage unless he is certain of the trustworthiness of the interpreter.

#1107 Even if a marriage has been entered into invalidly by reason of an impediment or defect of form, the consent given is presumed to persist until its withdrawal has been established.

Chapter V: The Form of the Celebration of Marriage

#1108 §1. Only those marriages are valid which are contracted in the presence of the local Ordinary or parish priest or of the priest or deacon delegated by either of them, who, in the presence of two witnesses, assists, in accordance however with the rules set out in the following canons, and without prejudice to the exceptions mentioned in cann. 144, 1112 §1, 1116 and 1127 §§2–3.

§2. Only that person who, being present, asks the contracting parties to manifest their consent and in the name of the Church receives it, is understood to assist at a marriage.

#1109 Within the limits of their territory, the local Ordinary and the parish priest by virtue of their office validly assist at the marriages not only of their subjects, but also of non-subjects, provided one or other of the parties is of the Latin rite. They cannot assist if by sentence or decree they have been excommunicated, placed under interdict or suspended from office, or been declared to be such.

#1110 A personal Ordinary and a personal parish priest by virtue of their office validly assist, within the confines of their jurisdiction, at the marriages only of those of whom at least one party is their subject.

#1111 §1. As long as they validly hold office, the local Ordinary and the parish priest can delegate to priests and deacons the faculty, even the general faculty, to assist at marriages within the confines of their territory.

§2. In order that the delegation of the faculty to assist at marriages be valid, it must be expressly given to specific persons; if there is question of a special delegation, it is to be given for a specific marriage; if however there is question of a general delegation, it is to be given in writing.

#1112 §1. Where there are no priests and deacons, the diocesan Bishop can delegate lay persons to assist at marriages, if the Conference of Bishops has given its prior approval and the permission of the Holy See has been obtained.

§2. A suitable lay person is to be selected, capable of giving instruction to those who are getting married, and qualified to conduct the marriage liturgy properly.

#1113 Before special delegation is granted, provision is to be made for all those matters which the law prescribes to establish the freedom to marry.

#1114 One who assists at a marriage acts unlawfully unless he has satisfied himself of the parties' freedom to marry in accordance with the law and, whenever he assists by virtue of a general delegation, has satisfied himself of the parish priest's permission, if this is possible.

#1115 Marriages are to be celebrated in the parish in which either of the contracting parties has a domicile or a quasi-domicile or a month's residence or, if there is a question of vagrants, in the parish in which they are actually residing. With the permission of the proper Ordinary or the proper parish priest, marriages may be celebrated elsewhere.

#1116   §1. If one who, in accordance with the law, is competent to assist, cannot be present or be approached without grave inconvenience, those who intend to enter a true marriage can validly and lawfully contract in the presence of witnesses only:

1) in danger of death;
2) apart from danger of death, provided it is prudently foreseen that this state of affairs will continue for a month.

§2. In either case, if another priest or deacon is at hand who can be present, he must be called upon and, together with the witnesses, be present at the celebration of the marriage, without prejudice to the validity of the marriage in the presence of only the witnesses.

#1117   The form prescribed above is to be observed if at least one of the parties contracting marriage was baptized in the Catholic Church or received into it and has not by a formal act defected from it, without prejudice to the provisions of can. 1127 §2.

#1118   §1. A marriage between Catholics, or between a Catholic party and a baptized non-Catholic, is to be celebrated in the parish church. By permission of the local Ordinary or of the parish priest, it may be celebrated in another church or oratory.

§2. The local Ordinary can allow a marriage to be celebrated in another suitable place.

§3. A marriage between a Catholic party and an unbaptized party may be celebrated in a church or in another suitable place.

#1119   Apart from a case of necessity, in the celebration of marriage those rites are to be observed which are prescribed in the liturgical books approved by the Church, or which are acknowledged by lawful customs.

#1120   The Conference of Bishops can draw up its own rite of marriage, in keeping with those usages of place and people which accord with the Christian spirit; it is to be reviewed by the Holy See, and it is without prejudice to the law that the person who is present to assist at the marriage is to ask for and receive the expression of the consent of the contracting parties.

#1121   §1. As soon as possible after the celebration of a marriage, the parish priest of the place of celebration or whoever takes his place, even if neither has assisted at the marriage, is to record in the marriage register the names of the spouses, of the person who assisted and of the witnesses, and the place and date of the celebration of the marriage; this is to be done in the manner prescribed by the Conference of Bishops or by the diocesan bishop.

§2. Whenever a marriage is contracted in accordance with can. 1116, the priest or deacon, if he was present at the celebration, otherwise the witnesses, are bound jointly with the contracting parties as soon as possible to inform the parish priest or the local Ordinary about the marriage entered into.

§3. In regard to a marriage contracted with a dispensation from the canonical form, the local Ordinary who granted the dispensation is to see to it that the dispensation and the celebration are recorded in the marriage register both of the Curia, and of the proper parish of the Catholic party whose parish priest carried out the inquiries concerning the freedom to marry. The Catholic spouse is obliged as soon as possible to notify that same Ordinary and parish priest of the fact that the marriage was celebrated, indicating also the place of celebration and the public form which was observed.

#1122   §1. A marriage which has been contracted is to be recorded also in the baptismal registers in which the baptism of the spouses was entered.

§2. If a spouse contracted marriage elsewhere than in the parish of baptism, the parish priest of the place of celebration is to send a notification of the marriage as soon as possible to the parish priest of the place of baptism.

#1123   Whenever a marriage is validated for the external forum, or declared invalid, or lawfully dissolved other than by death, the parish priest of the place of the celebration must be informed, so that an entry may be duly made in the registers of marriage and of baptism.

Chapter VI: Mixed Marriages

#1124—Without the express permission of the competent authority, marriage is prohibited between two baptized persons, one of whom was baptized in the Catholic Church or received into it after baptism and has not defected from it by a formal act, the other of whom belongs to a Church or ecclesial community not in full communion with the Catholic Church.

#1125   The local Ordinary can grant this permission if there is a just and reasonable cause. He is not to grant it unless the following conditions are fulfilled:

1) the Catholic party is to declare that he or she is prepared to remove dangers of defecting from the faith, and is to make a sincere promise to do all in his or her power in order that all the children be baptized and brought up in the Catholic Church;

2) the other party is to be informed in good time of these promises to be made by the Catholic party, so that it is certain that he or she is truly aware of the promise and of the obligation of the Catholic party;

3) both parties are to be instructed about the purposes and essential properties of marriage, which are not to be excluded by either contractant.

#1126   It is for the Conference of Bishops to prescribe the manner in which these declarations and promises, which are always required, are to be made, and to determine how they are to be established in the external forum, and how the non-Catholic party is to be informed of them.

#1127   §1. The provisions of can. 1108 are to be observed in regard to the form to be used in a mixed marriage. If, however, the Catholic party contracts marriage with a non-Catholic party of oriental rite, the canonical form of celebration is to be observed for lawfulness only; for validity, however, the intervention of a sacred minister is required, while observing the other requirements of law.

§2. If there are grave difficulties in the way of observing the canonical form, the local Ordinary of the Catholic party has the right to dispense from it in individual cases, having however consulted the Ordinary of the place of the celebration of the marriage; for validity, however, some public form of celebration is required. It is for the Conference of Bishops to establish norms whereby this dispensation may be granted in a uniform manner.

§3. It is forbidden to have, either before or after the canonical celebration in accordance with §1, another religious celebration of the same marriage for the purpose of giving or renewing matrimonial consent. Likewise, there is not to be a religious celebration in which the Catholic assistant and a non-Catholic minister, each performing his own rite, ask for the consent of the parties.

#1128   Local Ordinaries and other pastors of souls are to see to it that the Catholic spouse and the children born of a mixed marriage are not without the spiritual help needed to fulfill their obligations; they are also to assist the spouses to foster the unity of conjugal and family life.

#1129   The provisions of can. 1127 and 1128 are to be applied also to marriages which are impeded by the impediment of disparity of worship mentioned in can. 1086 §1.

Chapter VII: The Secret Celebration of Marriage

#1130   For a grave and urgent reason the local Ordinary may permit that a marriage be celebrated in secret.

#1131   Permission to celebrate a marriage in secret involves:
1) that the investigations to be made before the marriage are carried out in secret;
2) that the secret in regard to the marriage which has been celebrated is observed by the local Ordinary, by whoever assists, by the witnesses and by the spouses.

#1132   The obligation of observing the secret mentioned in can. 1131 n. 2 ceases for the local Ordinary if from its observance a threat arises of grave scandal or of grave harm to the sanctity of marriage. This fact is to be made known to the parties before the celebration of the marriage.

#1133   A marriage celebrated in secret is to be recorded only in a special register which is to be kept in the secret archive of the Curia.

Chapter VIII: The Effects of Marriage

#1134   From a valid marriage there arises between the spouses a bond which of its own nature is permanent and exclusive. Moreover, in Christian marriage the spouses are by a special sacrament strengthened and, as it were, consecrated for the duties and the dignity of their state.

#1135   Each spouse has an equal obligation and right to whatever pertains to the partnership of conjugal life.

#1136   Parents have the most grave obligation and the primary right to do all in their power to ensure their children's physical, social, cultural, moral and religious upbringing.

#1137   Children who are conceived or born of a valid or of a putative marriage are legitimate.

#1138   §1. The father is he who is identified by a lawful marriage, unless by clear arguments the contrary is proven.

§2. Children are presumed legitimate who are born at least 180 days after the date the marriage was celebrated, or within 300 days from the date of the dissolution of conjugal life.

#1139   Illegitimate children are legitimated by the subsequent marriage of their parents, whether valid or putative, or by a rescript of the Holy See.

#1140   As far as canonical effects are concerned, legitimated children are equivalent to legitimate children in all respects, unless it is otherwise expressly provided by the law.

Chapter IX: The Separation of the Spouses

Article 1: The Dissolution of the Bond

#1141   A marriage which is ratified and consummated cannot be dissolved by any human power or by any cause other than death.

#1142   A non-consummated marriage between baptized persons or between a baptized party and an unbaptized party can be dissolved by the Roman Pontiff for a just reason, at the request of both parties or of either party, even if the other is unwilling.

#1143   §1. In virtue of the Pauline privilege, a marriage entered into by two unbaptized persons is dissolved in favor of the faith of the party who received baptism, by the very fact that a new marriage is contracted by that same party, provided the unbaptized party departs.

§2. The unbaptized party is considered to depart if he or she is unwilling to live with the baptized party, or to live peacefully without offense to the Creator, unless the baptized party has, after the reception of baptism, given the other just cause to depart.

#1144   §1. For the baptized person validly to contract a new marriage, the unbaptized party must always be interpellated unbaptized whether:

1) he or she also wishes to receive baptism;
2) he or she at least is willing to live peacefully with the baptized party without offense to the Creator.

§2. This interpellation is to be done after baptism. However, the local Ordinary can for a grave reason permit that the interpellation be done before baptism; indeed he can dispense from it, either before or after baptism, provided it is established, by at least a summary and extra-judicial procedure, that it cannot be made or that it would be useless.

#1145 §1. As a rule, the interpellation is to be done on the authority of the local Ordinary of the converted party. A period of time for reply is to be allowed by this Ordinary to the other party, if indeed he or she asks for it, warning the person however that if the period passes without any reply, silence will be taken as a negative response.

§2. Even an interpellation made privately by the converted party is valid, and indeed it is lawful if the form prescribed above cannot be observed.

§3. In both cases there must be lawful proof in the external forum of the interpellation having been done and of its outcome.

#1146 The baptized party has the right to contract a new marriage with a Catholic:

1) if the other party has replied in the negative to the interpellation, or if the interpellation has been lawfully omitted;
2) if the unbaptized person, whether already interpellated or not, who at first persevered in peaceful cohabitation without offense to the Creator, has subsequently departed without just cause, without prejudice to the provisions of cann. 1144 and 1145.

#1147 However, the local Ordinary can for a grave reason allow the baptized party, using the Pauline privilege, to contract marriage with a non-Catholic party, whether baptized or unbaptized; in this case, the provisions of the canons on mixed marriages must also be observed.

#1148 §1. When an unbaptized man who simultaneously has a number of unbaptized wives, has received baptism in the Catholic Church, if it would be a hardship for him to remain with the first of the wives, he may retain one of them, having dismissed the others. The same applies to an unbaptized woman who simultaneously has a number of unbaptized husbands.

§2. In the cases mentioned in §1, when baptism has been received, the marriage is to be contracted in the legal form, with due observance, if need be, of the provisions concerning mixed marriages and of other provisions of law.

§3. In the light of the moral, social and economic circumstances of place and person, the local Ordinary is to ensure that adequate provision is made, in accordance with the norms of justice, Christian charity and natural equity, for the needs of the first wife and of the others who have been dismissed.

#1149 An unbaptized person who, having received baptism in the Catholic Church, cannot re-establish cohabitation with his or her unbaptized spouse by reason of captivity or persecution, can contract another marriage, even if the other party has in the meantime received baptism, without prejudice to the provisions of can. 1141.

#1150   In a doubtful matter the privilege of the faith enjoys the favor of the law.

Article 2: Separations While the Bond Remains

#1151   Spouses have the obligation and the right to maintain their common conjugal life, unless a lawful reason excuses them.

#1152   §1. It is earnestly recommended that a spouse, motivated by Christian charity and solicitous for the good of the family, should not refuse to pardon an adulterous partner and should not sunder the conjugal life. Nevertheless, if that spouse has not either expressly or tacitly condoned the other's fault, he or she has the right to sever the common conjugal life, provided he or she has not consented to the adultery, nor been the cause of it, nor also committed adultery.

§2. Tacit condonation occurs if the innocent spouse, after becoming aware of the adultery, has willingly engaged in a marital relationship with the other spouse; it is presumed, however, if the innocent spouse has maintained the common conjugal life for six months, and has not had recourse to ecclesiastical or to civil authority.

§3. Within six months of having spontaneously terminated the common conjugal life, the innocent spouse is to bring a case for separation to the competent ecclesiastical authority. Having examined all the circumstances, this authority is to consider whether the innocent spouse can be brought to condone the fault and not prolong the separation permanently.

#1153   §1. A spouse who occasions grave danger of soul or body to the other or to the children, or otherwise makes the common life unduly difficult, provides the other spouse with a reason to leave, either by a decree of the local Ordinary or, if there is danger in delay, even on his or her own authority.

§2. In all cases, when the reason for separation ceases, the common conjugal life is to be restored, unless otherwise provided by ecclesiastical authority.

#1154   When a separation of spouses has taken place, provision is always, and in good time, to be made for the due maintenance and upbringing of the children.

#1155   The innocent spouse may laudably readmit the other spouse to the conjugal life, in which case he or she renounces the right to separation.

Chapter X: The Validation of Marriage

Article 1: Simple Validation

#1156   §1. To validate a marriage which is invalid because of a diriment impediment, it is required that the impediment cease or be dispensed, and that at least the party aware of the impediment renews consent.

§2. This renewal is required by ecclesiastical law for the validity of the validation, even if at the beginning both parties had given consent and had not afterwards withdrawn it.

1157 The renewal of consent must be a new act of will consenting to a marriage which the renewing party knows or thinks was invalid from the beginning.

#1158 §1. If the impediment is public, consent is to be renewed by both parties in the canonical form, without prejudice to the provision of can. 1127 §3.

§2. If the impediment cannot be proved, it is sufficient that consent be renewed privately and in secret, specifically by the party who is aware of the impediment provided the other party persists in the consent given, or by both parties if the impediment is known to both.

#1159 §1. A marriage invalid because of a defect of consent is validated if the party who did not consent, now does consent, provided the consent given by the other party persists.

§2. If the defect of the consent cannot be proven, it is sufficient that the party who did not consent, gives consent privately and in secret.

§3. If the defect of consent can be proven, it is necessary that consent be given in the canonical form.

#1160 For a marriage which is invalid because of defect of form to become valid, it must be contracted anew in the canonical form, without prejudice to the provisions of can. 1127 §2.

Article 2: Retroactive Validation

#1161 §1. The retroactive validation of an invalid marriage is its validation without the renewal of consent, granted by the competent authority. It involves a dispensation from an impediment if there is one, and from the canonical form if it had not been observed, as well as a referral back to the past of the canonical effects.

§2. The validation takes place from the moment the favor is granted; the referral back, however, is understood to have been made to the moment the marriage was celebrated, unless it is otherwise expressly provided.

§3. A retroactive validation is not to be granted unless it is probable that the parties intend to persevere in conjugal life.

#1162 §1. If consent is lacking in either or both of the parties, a marriage cannot be rectified by a retroactive validation, whether consent was absent from the beginning or, though given at the beginning, was subsequently revoked.

§2. If the consent was indeed absent from the beginning but was subsequently given, a retroactive validation can be granted from the moment the consent was given.

#1163 §1. A marriage which is invalid because of an impediment or because of defect of the legal form, can be validated retroactively, provided the consent of both parties persists.

§2. A marriage which is invalid because of an impediment of the natural law or of the divine positive law, can be validated retroactively only after the impediment has ceased.

#1164   A retroactive validation may validly be granted even if one or both of the parties is unaware of it; it is not, however, to be granted except for a grave reason.

#1165   §1. Retroactive validation can be granted by the Apostolic See.

§2. It can be granted by the diocesan bishop in individual cases, even if a number of reasons for nullity occur together in the same marriage, assuming that for a retroactive validation of a mixed marriage the conditions of can. 1125 will have been fulfilled. It cannot, however, be granted by him if there is an impediment whose dispensation is reserved to the Apostolic See in accordance with can. 1078 §2, or if there is question of an impediment of the natural law or of the divine positive law which has now ceased.

Sample Forms

These forms illustrate some of the different approaches taken in various Tribunals throughout the United States. As you will see, some of the forms that ask about the marriage are much more detailed than others. Some use a question and answer format, others ask for a narrative, and still others ask for a narrative following a guideline provided by the Tribunal. In some Tribunals one petition can be adapted for use in a formal proceeding, a documentary proceeding, or even a dissolution proceeding.

Tribunals often provide basic general information sheets or brochures about annulments.

By reading the forms in this Appendix, you will see almost every major approach currently in use in the American Tribunals. There has been much discussion about adopting standardized forms throughout the Tribunals. This has not as yet been done.

Form A. General Information sheets

Form B. Petition for Annulment, with witness list and detailed, specific questions regarding marriage (question and answer format)

Form C. Petition for Annulment, including interviewing priest's assessments of merits and story of marriage (narrative format)

Form D. Preliminary Petition, including interviewing priest's recommendation to Tribunal and story of marriage (narrative format)

Form E. Request for Investigation of Marriage, combined with story of marriage (narrative format)

Form A GENERAL INFORMATION: THE NULLITY PROCEDURE

You are kindly asked carefully to read this entire page and the reverse side, detach it, and save it for future reference whenever any questions surface concerning your petition for annulment.

A marriage which has been celebrated with the proper formalities enjoys the favor of the law, and is presumed to be valid until proven otherwise.

The nullity of a marriage does not depend on the opinion of the parties themselves nor on the common opinion of others, but upon the facts as evidenced in court and determined by law.

Marriage is a communion of life which has been established by God. While the parties themselves contract the marriage, what they enter by their consent is an institution whose substance is not theirs to control or dissolve.

All marriages are presumed to be valid. The majority of them are in fact valid, and most are successful and enduring.

It must be recognized, however, that some marriages do prove to be unhappy, some so much so that they break down completely and the parties feel constrained to separate, often with anguish and great suffering to themselves and their children. But no mere breakdown of marriage, however agonizing and tragic, is itself proof that the marriage was not valid from the beginning. Without ambiguity it must be said that there are marriages which break down because one partner or the other neglects the clearly understood demands of married life and so fails culpably to fulfill those obligations.

On the other hand, the Church has always recognized another possibility, namely, that some marriages which fail have in fact been null and void from the beginning. That task of the Matrimonial Tribunal, after a thorough investigation and application of jurisprudence, is to pronounce upon the alleged nullity of such marriages.

A mere conjecture or opinion offered by a priest or layman that a marriage is invalid is not a professional and competent assessment nor does such a statement offer a reason for hope or guarantee that a marriage will be in fact declared invalid.

The time involved in the final disposition of a case will vary from case to case. It is possible that the processing of your case could take up to a year after the date of your *initial* interview at the *Tribunal Office.* No two marriages are alike and much depends on the cooperation of the various parties: i.e., parents, relatives, witnesses, priest advocate, as well as the type of information received. It is not fair to compare one case with another which externally may seem similar. Because of the number of active petitions much of our communication with you will be by mail. It is very important that you respond to any communications from this office immediately. Also, please inform this office of any address change subsequent to your initial petition.

You will be informed promptly of the final judgment of your case by your priest advocate and this Tribunal.

You are asked *not* to plan a marriage or to *set up a tentative wedding date* with a priest before the case is brought to a final disposition.

No petition for marriage nullity can be accepted until such time as the civil divorce is considered final under state law.

There is of necessity a certain amount of secretarial expense involved in any Tribunal procedure, just as there are essential expenses in the civil courts. These expenses are kept to a minimum and an account is forwarded to the petitioner when the case is complete. This is done whether the decision is affirmative or negative. While we realize that legal fees for a civil divorce are much higher than the annulments process, *the Tribunal incurs expenses which must be met and we ask your cooperation in this matter. Due consideration is given those who find it financially difficult. However, under no circumstances is the progress of a case contingent on the petitioner's financial ability or willingness to pay.*

The Tribunal handles all information with professional confidentiality. The petitioner, respondent and all witnesses are requested that they, in turn, not discuss any information they have given to the Tribunal with any third party.

A Declaration of Nullity of a previous marriage does not necessarily state that you are free to enter a second bond. There may be other impediments preventing you or your prospective spouse from entering a second marriage.

Form B   PETITION FOR ANNULMENT
For Tribunal Use Only
Case Number: _____
Grounds: _____
Petitioner: _____
Respondent: _____
Date Received: _____

Biography
Petitioner: _____ Birth Date: _____
(Maiden Name)
Address: _____ Birth Place _____
Phone: _____ Date of Baptism: _____
Religion now practiced: _____ Church & City: _____

Father's name: _____ Mother's name _____
Address: _____ Address: _____
Religion at time of birth: _____ Religion at time of birth: _____

Respondent: _____ Birth Date: _____
Address: _____ Birth Place: _____
Phone: _____ Date of Baptism: _____
Religion now practiced: _____ Church & City: _____

Father's name: _____ Mother's maiden name: _____
Address: _____ Address: _____
Religion at time of birth: _____ Religion at time of birth: _____

Marriage
Church: _____ Date: _____ City: _____
Name of Officiant: ____ Separations (number and duration): _____
Number of children: _____ If no children, why not? _____
For Catholics: If marriage did not take place in the Catholic Church,
was permission given to have it in some other church? _____
Last date of cohabitation: _____ Reconciliation efforts: _____
Does the Respondent know this petition is being filed? _____
Is the Respondent willing to cooperate? _____

Divorce
City: _____ County: _____ State: _____
Date: _____ Grounds: _____
Granted to: _____

Remarriage
If either party has remarried please give name of present spouse and
place and date of marriage: _____
Along with this petition, please obtain and forward the following:
1. Baptismal Certificate for each party.
2. Certificate of Marriage
3. Decree of Divorce
A. If the marriage is null because of a defect of form, have the petitioner complete the following affidavit of non-validation:
   I swear that at the time of our marriage _____ was a baptized

107

Catholic, and that our marriage was neither celebrated nor validated in the presence of a Catholic priest.

Petitioner _____

B. If this is a formal petition, complete the following:

Believing that my marriage was not valid, I am asking that the Tribunal conduct an investigation into the status of the marriage. I swear that the facts set forth in this petition are true and accurate, so help me God.

Date: _____ Petitioner: _____

Mandate

I hereby appoint the undersigned priest to act as my advocate in this case.

Petitioner _____

Acceptance

I hereby agree to act as advocate on behalf of the petitioner in this case.

Priest _____

Date _____ Parish _____

City _____

Preliminary Questions for the Petitioner

We suggest that you complete this questionnaire by yourself at home, at your convenience. From our experience in using this questionnaire, we have found that it is most beneficial if it is worked at over a period of time, answering only a few questions each day. That way you will have sufficient time to give detailed and complete answers, rather than simple "yes" and "no" type responses which are rarely helpful. If more space is needed for you to completely answer the questions, feel free to use extra sheets of paper but please number your answers.

Return this questionnaire and your answers to the priest who is working with you in presenting this petition.

Thank you for your cooperation.

_____
Name (Complete present legal name)

_____
Complete Maiden Name (If female)

_____
Street Address

_____
City   State   Zip Code

_____
Telephone Number (Including area code)

Your Occupation

List children of former marriage and their dates of birth. _____

Who was awarded custody of these children? Are all support and alimony stipulations of the civil divorce decree being complied with? If not, explain fully.

Petitioner's Background (Before the marriage)

1. Describe the type of family from which you came, indicating in detail any unhappiness in childhood and adolescence which stemmed from your family circle, i.e., unstable marriage of parents, dominance of one parent over the other, divorce of parents, special problems such as drinking, infidelity, overstrictness, significant deaths or illnesses or unhappy experiences, mental or emotional difficulties.

2. Describe to what extent religion was a significant part of your upbringing (i.e., frequency of church attendance, formal religious education, Confirmation, etc.).

3. Describe your present involvement and participation in the institutional Church. Why are you seeking a Church annulment?

4. How many brothers and sisters do you have? Are any of them married? Have any of them been divorced and remarried?

5. Describe your educational background (i.e., your attitude toward school, your achievements in school, the extent of your education—grade, high school, college, post-graduate).

6. Describe any dating experience before your former spouse, (approximate number of different persons dated, any serious romance, and the reason for its/their break-up).

7. Describe the role played by your family, friends, school, and church in the formation of your sexual understanding and attitude. Would you describe yourself as being well prepared for sexuality in marriage?

8. Describe any difficulties you may have had with alcohol, drugs, law enforcement agencies. How were these difficulties resolved?

9. Did you ever serve in the Armed Forces? If so, please give the dates and places of your assignments and the nature of your discharge.

10. Briefly evaluate your own personality profile (i.e., inferiority or superiority complex, sensitivity, judgment, temper, moodiness, selfishness, sense of confidence, responsibility, honesty, erratic or unpredictable conduct—your strengths and weaknesses).

11. Did your family and friends approve of your dating your former spouse? If not, why not?

Respondent's Background (Before marriage)

12. Evaluate the character of your former spouse's parents and give an estimate of their relationship and marriage. Did they approve of their son/daughter dating you? If not, why not?

13. If your former spouse has married brothers and/or sisters, please describe their marital relationships. Are there any divorces?

14. Describe the religious background of your former spouse and his/her participation and involvement in the institutional church.

15. Outline the educational background of your former spouse.

16. Describe your former spouse's history of dating (i.e., any serious romance and the reason for the break-up before your courtship).

17. Briefly indicate his/her attitudes toward sex and any related problems.

18. Trace any problems your former spouse had with alcohol, drugs, and/or law enforcement agencies. How were these problems resolved?

19. Did your former spouse ever serve in the Armed Forces? If so, please give the approximate dates of his/her assignments and the nature of his/her discharge.

20. Briefly give your own evaluation of your former spouse's personal strengths and weaknesses (i.e., inferiority or superiority complex, sensitivity, judgment, temper, moodiness, selfishness, sense of confidence, responsibility, honesty, erratic or unpredictable conduct, etc.).

Period of Courtship

21. When, where, and under what circumstances did you and your former spouse meet? What initially attracted you to him/her?

22. During the time you were dating one another, did you encounter any difficulties or misunderstandings serious enough to cause an interruption or break in the courtship? If so, describe these difficulties and the manner in which they were resolved.

23. During the time of your courtship, did either you or your former spouse date anyone else? If so, under what circumstances.

24. When and under what circumstances did you first begin to speak about marriage? Was there a formal engagement? If so, at whose suggestion did you become engaged?

25. Describe the role of sexuality in your courtship.

26. Was there a pregnancy involved before the marriage? If so, in what way did this pregnancy influence your decision to marry—that is, would you have married when you did had a pregnancy not been involved?

27. If there was a pregnancy, were alternatives other than marriage discussed between you and your former spouse and your families (i.e., adoption, birth outside of marriage, abortion)? Describe any such discussions.

28. Briefly describe the reaction of your families and friends to your courtship (i.e., the encouragement/discouragement of the continuation of your relationship, their sources of concern, their reaction to your engagement, their involvement in the wedding plans).

29. Describe the feelings that you and your former spouse had toward the having and raising of children.

30. Did both of you agree to the postponement of children in your marriage? If so, for what reasons was this decision made and what means were used to avoid children?

31. Did either you or your former spouse intend that you would never have children in the marriage? If so, please explain your answer.

32. Describe the attitudes of you and your former spouse toward your marriage as a permanent, life-long commitment to one another.

33. Discuss the attitudes of you and your former spouse toward divorce. Was divorce considered an ordinary and acceptable means of solving future marriage problems?

34. Did the two of you believe that civil divorce would free you, in conscience, to enter into another valid marriage?

35. Describe any discussions you and your former spouse had regarding fidelity in marriage. Did either one of you reserve the right to be unfaithful to each other in marriage? If fidelity was not discussed before your marriage, was the question of faithfulness ever discussed at any time in your relationship?

36. Did you and your former spouse receive instructions from a priest or minister concerning the essentials of marriage, that is, were both of you in agreement that your marriage was to be *life-long and permanent* and *family oriented*? During the course of these instructions did you and your former spouse disagree with the above-mentioned essentials? Please explain *fully* your answer.

37. If a priest prepared you for marriage, was a Pre-Marital Inventory (PMI) administered to you and your former spouse? If so, were there any areas of disagreement that surfaced on the PMI and were these areas adequately discussed before your marriage?

38. Did the person officiating at your marriage express any doubts or reservations concerning the advisability of your impending wedding? If so, please explain.

The Wedding

39. Describe the day of your wedding (i.e., your own feelings, the feelings of your former spouse, your family, and friends).

40. Were the immediate families and close friends of you and your for-

mer spouse present at the wedding ceremony and reception? If not, why not?

41. During those first few days after your marriage, did any difficulties arise between you and your former spouse (i.e., sexual, psychological, emotional, etc.)? If so, please explain.

Married Life

42. During the first year of marriage, where did the two of you live (i.e., with parents, in an apartment, in a single dwelling home)? Were you able to financially support yourselves?

43. During the first year or so of your marriage, were there any serious arguments, disagreements, or fights that stand out in your mind? If so, explain the nature of these.

44. Describe any personality traits, reactions, negative characteristics that you became aware of in your former spouse during the first year or so of marriage which were not apparent during the period of your courtship.

45. Describe to what extent you and your former spouse participated in the practice of religion during your marriage.

46. Describe the attitude each one of you had toward employment (i.e., relationships with employer and employees, job stability) and domestic chores.

47. How well did you and your former spouse fulfill responsibilities in general (i.e., toward each other, home life, etc.)? Explain.

48. If children were a part of your marriage, describe the attitude each of you had toward them, their care and discipline.

49. Briefly evaluate the ability of each one of you to communicate with the other (i.e., sharing with one another common interests, concerns, individual needs, etc.).

50. Would those persons close to you and your former spouse describe your marriage as being happy and off to a good start? If not, please explain.

51. Did either of you make impossible demands in any way on the other? Examples.

52. Describe how you and your former spouse related to in-laws. Did either set of parents interfere in your marriage?

53. Describe any significant physical and/or emotional mistreatment that was a part of your marriage.

54. Outline any problems during your former marriage that were related to alcohol, drugs, or law enforcement agencies.

55. Evaluate how you and your former spouse made use of leisure time.

56. Describe any important physical or psychological illnesses that either you or your former spouse encountered. Indicate if professional assistance was utilized.

57. Assess the importance of sexual expression in your marriage and sensitivity to each other's needs.

58. Evaluate how well you and your former spouse handled money. Were there common resources?

59. Describe how you and your former spouse spent a typical night at home.

60. Describe at what point in your marriage initial problems began to arise and indicate their cause.

61. Describe any separations that took place in your marriage (i.e., approximate dates, duration, cause, and manner of reconciliation).

62. Assess the involvement and utilization of any counselors and/or psychiatrists during the marriage (i.e., when, why, who, and by whom).

63. Briefly explain why you think and/or feel your marriage to your former spouse ended.

64. To what extent and in what manner were you, yourself, responsible for the difficulties that were encountered in your marriage?

65. Please describe any subsequent courtships and marriages of either you or your former spouse.

66. Describe and evaluate your present religious participation and involvement with the institutional Church.

67. Please mention below or on separate sheets of paper any information that has not already been covered that you think is important.

I, the undersigned Petitioner in the cause for an ecclesiastical annulment of my former marriage, do swear to the truthfulness of the statements I have made in this questionnaire, as well as to any subsequent testimony by me in the matter. I promise that I will not discuss with anyone, with the possible exception of the concerned priest, any questions put to me by the Tribunal or my testimony. I further swear that I will in no way coach anyone, neither the Respondent, parents, nor other witnesses connected with this case, as to how they should testify in the matter.

_____   _____
Date   Signature of the Petitioner

Other Marriages Attempted by You or Your Former Spouse

Yours   Former Spouse's
1) Name _____   1) Name _____
   Date of Marriage_____   Date of Marriage_____
   Place of Marriage _____   Place of Marriage _____
2) Name _____   2) Name _____
   Date of Marriage_____   Date of Marriage_____

113

Place of Marriage _____   Place of Marriage _____
3) Name _____   3) Name _____
Date of Marriage _____   Date of Marriage _____
Place of Marriage _____   Place of Marriage _____

Check the Appropriate Box:

☐ At this time I have no plans to marry.

☐ I intend to marry (name of betrothed _____)

Has he/she been married before? _____

☐ I am presently married.

Has present spouse been married before? _____

Witnesses to Be Contacted in This Case
(You should be assured of the willingness of the witnesses to testify in your marriage case.)

1) Name _____
   Address _____
   Telephone _____ Religion _____
   Why do you list this witness? _____
   _____

2) Name _____
   Address _____
   Telephone _____ Religion _____
   Why do you list this witness? _____
   _____

3) Name _____
   Address _____
   Telephone _____ Religion _____
   Why do you list this witness? _____
   _____

4) Name _____
   Address _____
   Telephone _____ Religion _____
   Why do you list this witness? _____
   _____

(Professional Witnesses)

1) Name _____ Type of Professional _____
   Address _____
   Telephone _____
   When Seen _____ By Whom _____

Form C PETITION FOR ANNULMENT AND REFERRAL SHEET

For Tribunal Use Only:
Protocol Number: _____
Date Received:_____
Procurator: _____
Church: _____
Jurisdiction of this Tribunal:
    a) Diocese of Petitioner: _____ of Respondent:_____
    b) Place of Marriage:_____
    c) Permission from another Diocese to Handle Case: _____

1. Petitioner: _____
   Address _____
   Telephone: Home: _____ Work:_____
   Date of Birth: _____ Place: _____
   Date of Baptism: _____ Place: _____
   Religion Baptized In: _____

2. Respondent: _____
   Address _____
   Telephone: Home: _____ Work:_____
   Date of Birth: _____ Place: _____
   Date of Baptism: _____ Place: _____
   Religion Baptized In: _____

3. Length of Dating Period: _____ of Engagement: _____

4. Marriage Ceremony:
   a) Date of Civil Marriage (if it applies):_____
   b) Date of Church Wedding:_____
   c) Name of Church: _____ Place: _____
   d) Priest (or Minister):_____ Place: _____
   e) Age of Petitioner at Wedding: Age of Respondent at Wedding:

_____   _____

5. During the Marriage:
   a) Length of Marriage:_____
   b) Number of Children born: _____
   c) Separations before final one, if any: _____
   d) Final Date of Cohabitation (not date of Divorce):_____

6. For the Advocate Only:
   Date of Divorce:_____ Place granted: _____

7. The story of my marriage, the causes of the final separation, and all of the events leading to it are attached to this Petition.

8. On what grounds can the validity of this marriage be questioned:

9. Witnesses or other evidence (such as letters) to support contentions of Petitioner. (Please give current names and addresses if possible.)

10. Other marriage(s) of Petitioner and Respondent (dates, names):

11. With this Petition, I am also submitting all documents needed, such as Baptismal Certificates for both parties (whether Catholic or not), the Marriage Certificate, Decree of Divorce, and the above-mentioned story of the marriage.

12. I hereby state that I leave it to the discretion of the Tribunal to appoint an approved Advocate to protect my rights and defend this cause before the Tribunal. I will undertake to cooperate with this Advocate in any way necessary to bring this case to a conclusion.

13. I understand that a fee is required for Tribunal expenses. I choose to pay $250_____/I would like to be billed at $25 monthly_____. I will also be responsible for other extraordinary expenses (telephone, testing, etc.), which may have to be incurred in completing this action.

_____   _____
Date   Signature of Petitioner

Priest-Procurator's Assessment of Petitioner's Merits:

Church Seal

_____
                                            Signature of Priest-Procurator

A Guideline for Writing the Story of Your Marriage (Only typewritten copies, please)

   I. Your Life Before Marriage
      A. Your Family Background
         1. What were your parents like and how did they get along?
         2. How far did they go in school and what did they do for a living?
         3. How did you get along with your mother and your father?
         4. How many brothers and sisters did you have and were you first, middle, or last?
         5. Did you have any unusual illnesses or other events in childhood?

      B. Your School Years
         1. How far did you go in school and how well did you do?
         2. How did you get along with your teachers?
         3. How old were you when you went on your first date alone with your date?

      C. Your Personality: Describe your good points and your bad points, moods, etc.

II. Your Spouse's Life Before Marriage

    A. Spouse's Family Background:

        1. What were the parents like and how did they get along?

        2. How far did they go in school and what did they do for a living?

        3. How did your spouse get along with mother and father?

        4. How many brothers and sisters were there and was your spouse first, middle, or last?

        5. Were there any unusual illnesses or other happenings in childhood?

    B. Spouse's School Years

        1. How far did he (she) go in school and how well did he do?

        2. How did he get along with his teachers?

        3. How old was he when he went on his first date alone with his date?

    C. Spouse's Personality: Describe his good and bad points, his usual mood, and anything else that will show what he was like as a person.

III. The Story of Your Marriage

    A. Courtship

        1. How did you meet? How long did you know each other before marriage?

        2. How often did you date and how long before marriage?

        3. Did you have sexual relations before marriage? Was there a pregnancy?

        4. How did the subject of marriage come up?

        5. How long before marriage were you engaged to be married?

        6. What was your attitude and your spouse's attitude toward having children?

        7. What did your parents and friends think of you two getting married?

    B. Wedding and Honeymoon

        1. What did you think and how did you feel the day of the wedding?

        2. What were the feelings of your spouse on the day of the wedding?

        3. Where did you go and how long did you stay on your honeymoon?

        4. When did you perform the marriage act together?

        5. Describe your feelings about the honeymoon.

    C. Your Married Life Together

        1. Describe your affection for each other and how often you expressed it in the marriage act (every night, twice a week, etc.). Were there any problems with sex?

        2. What was the attitude of each partner toward the work and

responsibilities of married life (earning a living, housework, cooking, caring for the children, etc.)?

3. Where did you live, and for how long, during the time you were married?

4. Who did the husband work for and how long at each job?

5. If the wife worked outside the home, who did she work for and how long?

6. What were the problems in your marriage?

7. Did you ever seek advice and counseling for the problems?

8. What caused any temporary separations, and how long did each last?

9. What was the real reason, the main reason, for the final separation?

10. What has each party done since the divorce (if remarried, how many times)?

Form D PRELIMINARY QUESTIONNAIRE
Preliminary Petition
I hereby submit the attached information, documents, and resume to the Diocesan Tribunal in order to begin the process of a Church Annulment.

_____
Petitioner

Statement of the Priest
I have reviewed the attached information and recommended this Petition to the Diocesan Tribunal.

_____
Priest or Deacon
_____
Date
_____
Parish
Parish Seal
_____
City

Please provide requested information for Sections A, B, and C on this form.

A. Petitioner
Your present name _____
Current address: Street ____ City ____ State _____ Zip _____
If woman, maiden name _ Phone number: Home__ Work __
Date of birth _____ Place of birth: City _____ State _____
Name of father_____ His religion _____
Present name of mother_____ Her religion _____
Have you been baptized? _____ If so, when? _____ Where? _____
In what religious denomination? _____
Your religion at time of marriage to respondent _____
Present religion _____ Current marital status _____
How many times have you been married (civilly or in Church) List all marriages of yourself, stating:
To whom (maiden name if woman), date, place

_____
_____
_____

If presently remarried, date and place of remarriage _____
Was current spouse or intended spouse ever married before? __
If so: When? _____ Where? _____ Before whom? _____

B. Respondent (Other Party to Marriage in Question)
Present Name _____
Current Address: Street _____ City ____ State _____ Zip _____

119

Telephone Number: Home _____ Work _____
If woman, maiden name_____
Date of birth _____ Place of birth: City _____ State _____
Was he/she ever baptized?_____ If so, when? ___ Where? _____
In what religious denomination? _____
How many times has he/she been married (civilly and/or in Church)?_____
To Whom (maiden name if woman) _____ Date_____ Place _____
His/Her current marital status _____

C. Marriage Under Investigation
Approximate length of courtship _____ Date of engagement _____
Date of marriage_____ Place: Church_____
   City _____ State _____
Approximate date of separation_____
Date and place of civil annulment/divorce (Final Decree)

_____
Grounds:_____
Ages at the time of wedding: (Yourself)_____ (Other Party) _____
Number of children born of this marriage Their names and dates of birth: _____
Length of time you and Respondent lived together (marriage to last separation) _____
Do you expect that the Respondent will cooperate with the Diocesan Tribunal in this case?
Yes _____ No _____ Maybe_____ Unknown _____
Please proceed to write your Resume, according to the outline on the next page.

NOTE: Petitioners are asked to attach to this form a narrative summary of their marriage using a format similar to that on pages 116–118.

Form E   REQUEST FOR INVESTIGATION OF MARRIAGE

NOTE: In this form the individual is asked to give a narrative summary of the marriage as on pages 116–118, and then the following is added, which has the effect of turning the background information guideline into a petition to investigate to determine if an annulment is in order.

  IV. Witnesses

      Submit a list of the names and addresses (and telephone numbers, if possible) of potential witnesses. These would be people who were knowledgeable about the marriage and the contracting parties. Family members often make good witnesses.

  V. Conclusion

      I hereby request the Tribunal of this diocese to investigate my former marriage to see if an annulment can be granted.

_____   _____
   The date   Your signature

Submit your narrative statement (story of your marriage), along with a copy of the marriage certificate and decree of divorce for the marriage to the office of the Tribunal of this diocese.

III

Volume of Formal Cases
Presented for Annulment

The listing below gives an indication of the Tribunal activity of the dioceses shown, but it does not reveal the number or percentage of petitions accepted or ultimately successful. Some dioceses with a relatively low total volume of cases have a very high percentage finally decided in favor of the Petitioner.

Ranking in Population	Diocese or Archdiocese	Approximate Population	Formal Petitions Filed (1981)	Ranking in Volume of Formal Petitions Filed†
1	Chicago	2,374,000	3,246	1
2	Los Angeles	2,304,000	933	9
3	Military Ordinariate	2,138,000	460	42
4	Boston	1,914,000	1,889	2
5	New York	1,839,000	405	48
6	Philadelphia	1,386,000	*	*
7	Newark	1,374,000	588	27
8	Brooklyn	1,372,000	1,236	6
9	Detroit	1,260,000	1,590	4
10	Rockville Centre	1,042,000	1,725	3
11	Cleveland	942,000	1,044	7
12	Pittsburgh	927,000	925	11
13	Miami	897,000	783	14
14	Buffalo	826,000	575	28
15	Hartford	794,000	685	17
16	Milwaukee	707,000	1,343	5
17	Providence	619,000	428	45
18	San Antonio	589,000	*	*
19	St. Paul–Minneapolis	573,000	273	70
20	St. Louis	543,000	*	*
21	New Orleans	525,000	461	41

VOLUME OF CASES PRESENTED FOR ANNULMENT

Ranking in Population	Diocese or Archdiocese	Approximate Population	Formal Petitions Filed (1981)	Ranking in Volume of Formal Petitions Filed†
22	Galveston-Houston	514,000	790	13
23	Cincinnati	506,000	944	8
24	Trenton	448,000	672	20
25	Baltimore	426,000	756	15
26	Joliet	411,000	458	43
27	Metuchen	411,000	*	*
28	Albany	409,000	646	23
29	Brownsville	402,000	136	120
30	Oakland	402,000	233	85
31	Washington, D.C.	397,000	337	55
32	Rochester	376,000	607	26
33	Syracuse	371,000	875	12
34	Scranton	365,000	228	87
35	Orange	365,000	467	40
36	Camden	352,000	*	*
37	Springfield, MA	352,000	652	21
38	San Francisco	352,000	647	22
39	Toledo	348,000	932	10
40	Green Bay	344,000	565	30
41	Fall River	340,000	124	126
42	Worcester	337,000	487	37
43	Bridgeport	331,000	306	64
44	San Diego	330,000	569	29
45	Paterson	327,000	270	71
46	Santa Fe	323,000	163	111
47	Lafayette, LA	320,000	701	16
48	St. Petersburg	311,000	373	51
49	Corpus Christi	311,000	203	92
50	Fresno	311,000	325	56
51	Denver	309,000	503	34
52	Portland, OR	301,000	310	61
53	San Jose	301,000	*	*
54	Youngstown	291,000	437	44
55	Manchester	291,000	560	31
56	Portland, ME	272,000	498	35
57	Seattle	270,000	634	24
58	Allentown	263,000	410	46
59	Phoenix	263,000	615	25
60	San Bernardino	249,000	345	53
61	Peoria	246,000	292	66
62	El Paso	245,000	187	100
63	Dubuque	238,000	678	18
64	Rockford	236,000	*	*
65	La Crosse	231,000	398	50
66	Erie	226,000	316	59
67	Tucson	225,000	129	122
68	Greenburg	225,000	198	95
69	Madison	221,000	185	103

Ranking in Population	Diocese or Archdiocese	Approximate Population	Formal Petitions Filed (1981)	Ranking in Volume of Formal Petitions Filed†
70	Louisville	212,000	36	154
71	Lansing	209,000	678	19
72	Honolulu	209,000	166	107
73	Omaha	208,000	234	83
74	Harrisburg	206,000	255	80
75	Indianapolis	202,000	187	99
76	Norwick	199,000	210	91
77	Columbus	195,000	*	*
78	Gary	194,000	82	145
79	Springfield, IL	186,000	191	98
80	Orlando	183,000	550	33
81	Baton-Rouge	181,000	212	90
82	Arlington, VA	179,000	*	*
83	Dallas	178,000	487	36
84	Saginaw	173,000	272	71
85	Ogdensburg	169,000	558	32
86	Philadelphia (Ukrainian)	168,000	36	155
87	Burlington	158,000	183	105
88	St. Cloud	155,000	184	104
89	Altoona-Johnstown	153,000	85	143
90	Grand Rapids	153,000	338	54
91	Pittsburg (Byzantine)	152,000	36	153
92	Fort Wayne– South Bend	152,000	262	75
93	Kansas City, KS	147,000	402	49
94	Kansas City– St. Joseph	144,000	127	123
95	Reno–Las Vegas	144,000	200	95
96	Houma-Thibodaux	133,000	90	141
97	Monterey	130,000	66	147
98	Austin	128,000	244	82
99	Winona	127,000	256	79
100	Belleville	122,000	320	58
101	Wilmington	121,000	187	101
102	Stockton	117,000	98	137
103	Richmond	115,000	471	38
104	Sioux City	113,000	154	118
105	Davenport	111,000	295	65
106	Atlanta	110,000	471	39
107	Pueblo	109,000	259	78
108	Wheeling- Charleston	106,000	124	127
109	Covington	104,000	370	52
110	Sioux Falls	100,000	160	114
111	Fort Worth	99,000	277	68
112	Wichita	99,000	160	115

VOLUME OF CASES PRESENTED FOR ANNULMENT

Ranking in Population	Diocese or Archdiocese	Approximate Population	Formal Petitions Filed (1981)	Ranking in Volume of Formal Petitions Filed†
113	Fargo	99,000	265	74
114	Passaic	97,000	28	157
115	Duluth	96,000	185	102
116	Kalamazoo	96,000	201	94
117	Beaumont	94,000	274	69
118	Superior	93,000	88	142
119	Marquette	90,000	163	112
120	Santa Rosa	90,000	106	136
121	Evansville	90,000	148	119
122	Lake Charles	89,000	316	60
123	Gaylord	87,000	164	109
124	Lafayette, IN	86,000	107	135
125	Jefferson City	86,000	309	63
126	Des Moines	83,000	123	128
127	Alexandria–Shreveport	83,000	134	121
128	Amarillo	81,000	406	47
129	Oklahoma City	80,000	324	57
130	Bismarck	79,000	45	150
131	Boise	77,000	222	88
132	Spokane	75,000	245	81
133	New Ulm	74,000	95	139
134	San Angelo	73,000	121	130
135	Nashville	72,000	287	67
136	St. Augustine	72,000	160	113
137	Lincoln	69,000	80	146
138	Cheyenne	68,000	233	84
139	Charleston	66,000	216	89
140	Great Falls–Billings	66,000	171	106
141	Helena	65,000	165	108
142	Salina	62,000	231	86
143	Salt Lake City	62,000	122	129
144	Little Rock	61,000	271	72
145	Mobile	60,000	203	93
146	Gallup	58,000	43	151
147	Yakima	58,000	195	97
148	Birmingham	56,000	114	132
149	Savannah	55,000	163	110
150	Grand Island	54,000	260	76
151	Steubenville	54,000	260	76
152	Biloxi	53,000	96	138
153	Springfield–Cape Girardeau	52,000	309	62
154	Charlotte, NC	51,000	*	*
155	Owensburg	50,000	40	152
156	Tulsa	49,000	270	73
157	Raleigh	49,000	95	140

Ranking in Population	Diocese or Archdiocese	Approximate Population	Formal Petitions Filed (1981)	Ranking in Volume of Formal Petitions Filed†
158	Memphis	48,000	157	117
159	Stamford	47,000	5	161
160	Pensacola-Tallahassee	44,000	*	*
161	Crookston	44,000	120	131
162	Jackson	44,000	159	116
163	Rapid City	40,000	112	133
164	Dodge City	39,000	108	134
165	Parma	36,000	33	156
166	St. Maron	34,000	47	149
167	Baker	26,000	23	159
168	Newton (Melkite)	23,000	54	148
169	Anchorage	21,000	81	145
170	Fairbanks	15,000	25	158
171	Juneau	5,000	9	160

*No statistics available.
†Because these statistics were not available for the ten dioceses with asterisks, the ranking for formal annulments is necessarily based only on the 161 dioceses reporting formal petitions filed.

BIBLIOGRAPHY

Alesandro, John A. "Law and Renewal: A Canon Lawyer's Analysis of the Revised Code." *Proceedings*, Canon Law Society of America, 1983, pp. 1–40.

"Annulments by U.S. Catholics at Peak." *New York Times*, January 6, 1982, p. 12.

Arella, Gerald J. "Approaches to Tribunal Practice—A Resume of Ten Years Experience." *The Jurist*, Vol. 31, pp. 489–505.

_____. "Case for the Marriage Court." *America*, October 21, 1982, pp. 316–20.

Barnhiser, Judith, O.S.A. "Clarifications Concerning Certain Questions About Tribunals in the United States of America." *The Jurist*, Vol. 41, Part 1, 1981, pp. 189–218.

Bass, Howard L. and Rein, M.L. *Divorce or Marriage: A Legal Guide*. Englewood Cliffs, N.J.: Prentice-Hall, 1976.

Bernhard, Jean. "The Evolution Of Matrimonial Jurisprudence: The Opinion Of A French Canonist." *The Jurist*, Vol. 41, Part 2, pp. 105–116.

Bosler, Ray. "Insanity Use Increases." *The Witness* (Dubuque), May 9, 1982, p. 10.

Callahan, Parnell, J. *The Law of Separation and Divorce*. 4th ed. Dobbs Ferry, N.Y.: Oceana, 1979.

Castelli, James. *What the Church Is Doing for Divorced and Remarried Catholics*. Chicago: Claretian Publications, 1978.

"Catholic Divorce?" *Time*, February 25, 1980, p. 40.

Catoir, John T. "When the Courts Don't Work." *America*, October 9, 1971, pp. 254-257.

_____. "Judging the Courts." *America*, November 4, 1972, p. 350.

_____. *Catholics and Broken Marriage*. Notre Dame, Ind.: Ave Maria, 1979.

"Children, Conscience and a Marriage Declared Null." *St. Anthony Messenger*, September 1981, pp. 45-46.

Doherty, Dennis. *Divorce and Remarriage: Resolving a Catholic Dilemma*. St. Meinrad, Ind.: Abbey Press, 1974.

Doyle, Kenneth J. "New Code Has Annulment Change: Expands Lay Role." *The Witness* (Dubuque), November 8, 1981, p. 10.

Doyle, Thomas P. "The Church and Marital Breakdown." *Listening*, Winter 1980, pp. 54-62.

Francis, Phillip. *Legal Status of Women*. 2nd ed. Dobbs Ferry, N.Y.: Oceana, 1978.

Goodnow, Kay London. *Credo*. Prairie Village, Kansas: Credo, 1980.

Graham, George P. "Catholics, Divorce, and Annulment." *USA Today*, January 1979, pp. 47-48.

Greeley, Andrew. "Church Unaware of Family Woes." *The Witness*, (Dubuque), April 3, 1980, p. 4.

_____. "Revised Code Will Be Non-Event." *The Witness* (Dubuque), March 26, 1981, p. 4.

Green, Thomas J. "Psychological Grounds for Church Annulments: Changing Canonical Practice." *Catholic Mind*, February 1979, pp. 38-49.

Hebblethwaite, Peter. "John Paul Urges Brakes on Annulment Process." *National Catholic Reporter*, February 15, 1980, p. 6.

Hudson, J. Edward, comp. *Handbook II for Marriage Nullity Cases*. Ottawa: St. Paul University, 1980.

James, Edward. "Marriage Tribunals: Another Viewpoint." *America*, May 5, 1979, pp. 370-371.

Johnson, John. "A Proposed In Iure Section for the New Statute of Fraud." *The Jurist*, Vol. 42, pp. 215-228.

Kelleher, Stephen J. *Divorce and Remarriage for Catholics*. Garden City, N.Y.: Doubleday, 1973.

_____. "Divorced Catholics: Starting Fires in a Cold Church." *U.S. Catholic*, June 6, 1978, pp. 6-12.

_____. "Looking Back, Looking Ahead." *America*, November 18, 1978, pp. 355-357.

_____. "Catholic Annulments: A Dehumanizing Process." *Commonweal*, June 10, 1977, pp. 363-368.

Kuchler, Frances W. *Law of Engagement and Marriage*. 2nd ed. Dobbs Ferry, N.Y.: Oceana, 1978.

Lavin, Martin E. "Canonical Equity Applied to Moral Certainty and to Worth of Expert Testimony." *The Jurist*, Vol. 35, pp. 316-322.

Lebel, Robert Roger. "Genetic Grounds for Annulment." *The Jurist*, Spring & Fall, 1976, pp. 317-327.

Maher, John. "Canon Lawyers Defend Marriage Court Practices." *The Witness* (Dubuque), February 19, 1981, p. 10.

"Married in the Church After Three Divorces?" *St. Anthony Messenger*, December 1981, p. 46.

Marx, Adolph. *The Declaration of Nullity of Marriages Contracted Outside the Church*. Washington, D.C.: Catholic University of America Press, 1943.

May, William E. "Marriage, Divorce and Remarriage." *The Jurist*, Spring & Fall, 1977, pp. 266-286.

Morrisey, Francis G. "The Impediment of Ligamen and Multiple Marriages." *The Jurist*, Vol. 40, Part 2, 1980, pp. 406-418.

Mulloy, John J. "Annuling the Institution of Marriage?" *The Wanderer*, February 11, 1982, p. 4.

_____. "By Reason of Insanity or Other Psychic Anomalies." *The Wanderer*, March 4, 1982.

Mungovan, Mary. "It's Not Who You Know, But Where You Go." *U.S. Catholic*, June 1978, pp. 13-18.

"New Statistics Reveal Facts About Annulments." *The Witness* (Dubuque), February 19, 1981, p. 10.

Pfnausch, Edward G. "The Question of Tribunals." *America*, November 18, 1978, pp. 352-354.

Pilpel, Harriet F. and Zavin, Theodora. *Your Marriage and the Law*. New York: Rinehart & Co., 1952.

Pospishil, Victor J. *Divorce and Remarriage: Towards a New Catholic Teaching*. New York: Herder & Herder, 1967.

Premo, Blanche, L. "The Pathos of Annulment." *Listening*, Winter 1980, pp. 64-70.

Risk, James E. *Marriage-Contract and Sacrament: A Manual of the Laws of the Catholic Church on Marriage for the Use of American Lawyers*. Chicago: Callaghan, 1957.

Ruzick, Kenneth J. "Competence, Nullity of the Acts, and the Appeal Process: A Look at the Procedural Law of the New Code." *Proceedings*, Canon Law Society of America, 1983, pp. 105–120.

Salzman, Leon. "Catholic Annulment and Civil Divorce." *America*, May 5, 1978, pp. 367–369.

Sheed, F. J. *Nullity of Marriage*. New ed. New York: Sheed & Ward, 1959.

Siegle, Bernard A. *Marriage Today: A Commentary on the Code of Canon Law*. 3rd ed. Staten Island, N. Y., Alba , 1979.

"Slow Annulment." *Time*, November 9, 1981, p. 59.

Spain, Michael, "Annulment Review Boards 'Not Punitive,' " *National Catholic Reporter*, March 4, 1983, p. 19.

Tierney, Terence E. *Annulment: Do You Have a Case?* Staten Island, N.Y.: Alba House, 1978.

True, Michael and Young, James. "Divorce and Remarriage." *Commonweal*, November 22, 1974, pp. 185–190.

Van Der Poel, Cornelius J. "Influences of an 'Annulment Mentality,' " *The Jurist*, Vol. 40, Part 2, 1980, pp. 384–399.

"Vatican Annulments Are Enormously Complicated, Rarely Granted—and Very Expensive." *People*, July 28, 1980, p. 31.

Walsh, Sr. Mary. "Let's Allow Nonsacramental Second Marriages," *U.S. Catholic*, September 1981, pp. 14–19.

Wilcox, Robert. "Healing Divorced Catholics." *Catholic Digest*, September 1982.

Winiarski, Mark. "Divorce, Remarriage Woes Vex U.S. Church." *National Catholic Reporter*, December 29, 1978, pp. 1 and 7.

Wrenn, Lawrence G. *Divorce and Remarriage in the Catholic Church*. New York: Newman, 1973.

——————————. *Annulments*. 3rd ed. Toledo, Ohio: Canon Law Society of America, 1978.

——————————. *Decisions*. Toledo, Ohio: Canon Law Society of America, 1982.

Young, James J. "Six Factors in a Climate of Change." *America*, November 18, 1978a, pp. 347–351.

——————————. *Ministering to the Divorced Catholic*. Ramsey, N.J.: Paulist Press, 1978b.